Silent Screams and Hidden Cries

An Interpretation of Artwork by Children from Violent Homes

Silent Screams and Hidden Cries

An Interpretation of Artwork by Children from Violent Homes

by

Agnes Wohl, C.S.W., A.C.S.W.
Bobbie Kaufman, M.P.S., ATR

Under the auspices of the
Coalition for Abused Women, Inc.

BRUNNER/MAZEL *Publishers* • New York

Library of Congress Cataloging in Publication Data

Wohl, Agnes.
  Silent screams and hidden cries.

  Bibliography: p.
  Includes indexes.
  1. Children of abused wives. 2. Abused children.
  3. Children as artists. 4. Draw-a-person test.
  5. Draw-a-family test. 6. House-tree-person technique.
  I. Kaufman, Bobbie. II. Coalition for
  Abused Women (Nassau County, N.Y.)
  III. Title. [DNLM: 1. Art. 2. Child Abuse.
  3. Family. 4. Projective Technics–in infancy
  & childhood. 5. Violence. WS 105.5.E8 W846s]
  RJ507.F35W65   1985   618.92'89'075   85-6652
  ISBN 0-87630-392-0

Published by
BRUNNER/MAZEL, Inc.
19 Union Square West
New York, N.Y. 10003

Manufactured in the United States of America

10 9 8 7

CONTENTS

ABOUT THE COALITION

The Coalition for Abused Women, Inc. (CAW), a non-profit agency, began as a volunteer hotline in 1976 in response to the lack of services to victims of domestic violence in the community. During the past few years the Coalition has also established the only state-certified shelter in Nassau County, New York, a volunteer Safe Home network, a model for legal-social work assistance to victims of abuse, a program of technical assistance and training for professionals, an advocacy network of community organizations for domestic violence legislations, and a visible, substantial service agency in the community. The County Executive has honored the Coalition in his annual proclamation of Domestic Violence Prevention and Awareness Week in each of the last four years. In addition, CAW's work is well recognized and supported by local legislators.

The goals of the Coalition are to reduce family violence, offer assistance to battered women and their families, and increase the responsiveness of public agencies, systems, and the community to victims of abuse. CAW has several organizational components to carry out these goals including: a Family Abuse Center with hotline, advocacy, and counseling services; a Legal Services Project; the Safe Home for Abused Families; and a Community Education Project. The agency is funded by both public and private sources and works closely with many private and public institutions throughout the county.

ABOUT THE AUTHORS

Bobbie Kaufman, a Registered Art Therapist, received her master's degree in Art Therapy and Creative Development from Pratt Institute in Brooklyn, New York, in 1977. Ms. Kaufman decided to study the creative arts therapies after her own experience taught her that the use of creative expression not only facilitates the release of emotions, but also fosters communication, self-integration, and self-awareness.

Bobbie Kaufman, a poet and stone carver in her spare time, maintains a practice in consultation and in psychotherapy in Centerport, New York, where she works with children, adults, couples, and families. She is also on the adjunct faculty of Hofstra University, Hempstead, New York, and is a consultant to the Coalition for Abused Women and to Empire State College, Westbury, New York. She is a guest lecturer for the Greater Alcoholism Council of New York City; Adelphi University, Garden City, New York; New York Institute of Technology; and various voluntary agencies.

Ms. Kaufman, who is also employed as the Long Island Regional Training Coordinator for the New York State Office of Mental Health, sees her professional role as one of helping to build bridges—between people, between organizations, and, particularly, between the internal factions within the individual and the family.

Agnes Wohl, a New York State Certified Social Worker, received her master's degree in Social Work in 1981 from Adelphi

University, New York. She is a member of the Academy of Certified Social Workers and is also a New York State Certified School Psychologist, having received her Advanced Certificate from City College, New York, in 1984. She is an adjunct lecturer in the psychology department of Baruch College, New York City, and has led a variety of workshops in community agencies, including such topics as Single Parenthood, The Effects of Divorce on Children, Techniques of Child Therapy, Child Development, Interpretations of Children's Artwork, and Children Living With Domestic Violence.

Ms. Wohl worked as a Social Worker-Family Therapist at Leake and Watts Children's Home, Inc., Preventive Foster Care Unit, in the East Bronx. She was employed full time with the Coalition for Abused Women as the Child and Family Psychotherapist at their Safe Home for Abused Families. Presently, she is employed by Queens Child Guidance in their Abuse Prevention Program. She also does evaluations of children as an independent consultant, and will be starting a private practice as a child psychotherapist.

ACKNOWLEDGMENTS

We are grateful to the staff, administration, and Board of Directors of the Coalition for Abused Women, Inc. (CAW), for their support and assistance throughout the development of this book.

In particular, we want to thank Sandy Oliva, Executive Director; Alberta Rubin, Director of Client Services; Beth Rosenthal, Former Safe Home Supervisor; Gina Trezza, Art Therapist; Helen Easley, Hot Line Supervisor; Myrna Van Bergen, Advocate; Lynn Cugini, Community Educator; Phoebe Alterman and Beth Smith, Board Members. Bobbie Kaufman wishes to personally thank her husband, Mal Dankner, and her children, Janice, Michelle, Larry, and Allison, for their understanding and patience; Agnes Wohl thanks her partner, Gary Bernstein, for his support during this two-year process.

Special thanks must also go to the families at the Safe Home who participated in this project, and whose names have been changed to protect their identities.

CAW wishes to acknowledge the support of the New York State Department of Social Services and the State of New York under a grant from which portions of this book were written.

The opinions, results, findings, and/or interpretations of data contained herein are the responsibility of the Coalition for Abused Women, Inc., and do not necessarily represent the opinions, interpretations, or policy of the New York State Department of Social Services or the State of New York. The Department expressly reserves the right to a royalty-free, nonexclusive, and irrevocable license to reproduce, publish, distribute, or otherwise use, in perpetuity, any and all of this material.

Agnes Wohl
Bobbie Kaufman

INTRODUCTION AND
PERSPECTIVE

This book presents us with a probing study of a number of the enduring and elemental aspects of life: children; family; injustice; lust; cruelty; sexuality; incest; innocents who have been betrayed; dramas which have been in motion since the birth of civilization; and the inner human process that surges under the conventional surface in the unconscious.

Writing about these concerns can often sink to the level of sensationalism. But the authors' tone is, and stays, thoughtful, compassionate, investigative, and insightful. What emerges is not so much shocking as a vivid portrait of families suffering angst and fevers.

At the same time, sensitive and poignant vignettes convey the story of the awful effects on these youngsters, the victims of brutality witnessed and of brutality received. The writers first chart and then take us behind the crescendo of sorrow and self-protection. The little girls are caught in the process of identifying with the victim-mother and, barring therapeutic intervention, growing up to be victims of batterers themselves; the little boys are caught in identifying with the aggressor-father, donning the enemy's cloak to put themselves out of harm's way and taking the pathway, thus, to become batterers when they marry.

Readers might, as they read the compelling material of this book, orient themselves to look for the subtleties of how the family influences the child, and how the child then assumes a certain role in order to sustain the family. In addition, it is important to realize that the mates live in the marriage, and this relationship lives in each mate. Echoes are heard from one to the other. This is also true of child and family.

Thus, each polarity actually helps to shape its corresponding other polarity, even if unconsciously; therefore, if we can perceive the inner process of one, we can also discover insights into the other. The projective drawings of the subjects in this book reflect powerful forces and powerful effects. We see in all of this, if we look, how husband and wife, how parents and child are somehow tied to the counterpart in the other, each sustaining and promoting the other, each at risk if the other should fail in his or her already assumed role.

As a guide to this book, there is something else to which I would draw the reader's attention: the authors' use of certain tools, skillfully employed, to enable them to probe below the surface of children, to uncover what children *will* not tell us or what they *cannot* tell us because they dare not reveal certain of the feelings even to themselves, and to see what cannot ordinarily be seen. These tools are projective drawings.

When children draw spontaneously, they choose, among their most frequent content, to draw houses and trees and people. It is upon this personal choice that a more formalized approach, the House-Tree-Person (HTP) Test (Buck, 1981) was devised.

A No. 2 pencil and a sheet of paper are handed to the subject. A drawing of a house is requested, with the longer axis of the sheet placed horizontally before the subject. Drawings of a tree and person, in turn, are then obtained on separate sheets of paper with the longer axis placed vertically. The subject is asked to draw as well as he or she can, but is not told what kind of house, tree, and person to draw.

If the subject protests that he or she is not an artist, he or she is assured that we are interested not in artistic ability, but rather, in how that child does things. Any questions he or she asks are reflected back in such a way as to indicate that there is no right or wrong method of proceeding but that the child may do the drawing in any manner he or she wishes.

After the child draws the person, he or she is handed another sheet of paper and this time told to draw a person of the opposite sex to that of the first person drawn. In addition, the subject may be asked to draw the most unpleasant thing he or she can think of, or to draw a person in the rain, the latter tapping the sense of self when in stress situations. Then the drawings of a house, a tree, and a person of each sex are repeated, this time in crayon. With children, we also ask for a drawing of a family (Hammer, 1980).

Burns (1982) had modified the Draw-A-Family by adding an action — or, as he terms it, a kinetic — dimension. The instructions to the subject are simple: Draw everyone in your family *doing something*. The results, however, are often rich and dramatic, bringing forth, for instance, a child's panic in response to an alcoholic father, feelings of isolation in a rejecting family, or massive withdrawal from threatening others in the household. Aspects elicited by this projective technique regarding self and regarding family interactions are those of intimacy or distance, emotional tone in the family, pleasantness or unpleasantness in the home setting, and feelings of who is closest to whom. Are family members interacting, or touching, or are they isolated from each other? Which member is facing which other member? Are certain family members, or the self-figure, using one or another activity to show off, or hide, or lure, or gain protection from a parent or sibling? Which family member is dominant and which secondary? Which are happy, sad, suffering, bored, cruel, rigid, detached, enraged, subservient, or trusting? Are members of the family comfortable or strained with each other, and what are their messages towards each other?

To further elicit cues to "reading" a subject's family drawing, Burns suggests that clinicians ask themselves (and, I would add, that they ask the subject): What if the drawing came to life? What would be happening? Who would go? Who would stay? Who would nurture? Who would hate? Who would love? What feelings are flowing from the father, or mother, or siblings, or self?

The projective drawing process, as I've pointed out elsewhere (Hammer, 1980), can be conceptualized as follows: The drawing page serves as a canvas upon which children may project a glimpse of their inner world, their traits and attitudes, their behavioral characteristics, their personality strengths and weaknesses. Children find it easier to communicate through drawings than through the verbal projective techniques much that is important to them and much that troubles them.

Both children and primitive people consistently draw elements that they consider essential, while they drop out others that do not concern them. They then include aspects that are known to be there but are not visible. The goal, thus, of both child and primitive is not "objective realism" but what Luquet (1913) called "mental realism."

In terms of expressive aspects, children's movements have diagnostic potential whether they are gross (as in the play therapy room) or confined (as on the drawing page). A child may withdraw into a corner of the room or sit on the edge of the chair, as though he or she were ready to run away; if the child is given a big sheet of paper, he may follow suit by drawing cautiously in one corner of the page only. At the other extreme, a child may sit at a table as though he wished to occupy the whole space, showing no consideration for the other children there. No paper is big enough for him, either, and his drawings expand beyond the drawing sheet. Projective drawings thus "capture" and record expressive movements on paper.

Whereas the aggressive child draws big, dangerous arms with long fingers, the inadequate or withdrawn child forgets to draw any hands at all, as though the subject had not experienced helping hands when he or she needed them, or as if hands were guilty things that may be used to do something that is labeled as taboo in our culture.

As a reflection of their virility strivings, delinquent children frequently draw soldiers or cowboys as symbols of status attained through the use of force and aggression.

With many children, drawings assume the character of an overemphasized, exaggerated portrait of strength or importance. Within the normal range, children and adolescents tend to draw themselves as more forceful, more glamorous, bigger, or older than they actually are, a depiction indicative of their own wishes about themselves. They put into the picture a promise of that reality which they desire.

In addition to the physical self, the subject projects a picture of the psychological self into his drawing of the person. Subjects of adequate or superior height may draw a tiny figure, with arms dangling rather helplessly away from the sides and a beseeching facial expression. Here the subjects are projecting their psychological view of themselves as tiny, insignificant, helpless, dependent, and in need of support, their physical selves notwithstanding. Other examples are: the toppling person, losing equilibrium, offered by a preschizophrenic child; the mannequin-like clothes dummy suggesting feelings of depersonalization; the adolescent's drawing of a person carrying a baseball bat in one hand, a tennis racket in the other, and wearing a mustache on his lip, revealing by his yearning for so many badges of virility his underlying feelings of inadequacy in this area; the drawing of a clown as a fusion of the child's attempts to depict the harmlessness of his instinctual impulses and the secondary use of this concept as an attention-getting maneuver; the reduced energy and drive suggested by the person drawn slumped into a chair or sitting on the curb of the street. All these themes support the thesis that the drawing of a person may represent a psychological self-portrait.

Armed with the knowledge that people's deeper needs color their creative efforts and show an affinity for speaking in pictorial images, clinicians have at their disposal a rapidly and easily administered technique for eliciting submerged levels of feelings. Basically, the subjects' relative emphasis of different elements within their drawings, in addition to their global drawing performance, tells us a good deal of what matters to them, what it does to them, and what they do about it.

Thus, it is on the basis of such projective drawing assessment that the authors of this book draw the profile of the children studied, profiles touchingly rendered and sharply realized.

In drawing their study to a close, the authors extend their distilled insights, with clinical sophistication, to recommendations regarding: 1) early detection of traumatization in children; and 2) treatment of such children and their families to assist these lost youngsters and floundering families to take hold, once more, of their lives.

Emanuel F. Hammer, Ph.D.
Clinical Professor
Institute for Advanced Psychological Studies
Adelphi University;
Director
American Projective Drawing Institute

Silent Screams and Hidden Cries

An Interpretation of Artwork by
Children from Violent Homes

CHAPTER 1

ABOUT THE CHILDREN
AND THEIR ARTWORK

The Safe Home for Abused Families, established under the Coalition for Abused Women, Inc., has provided safe housing, and psychotherapeutic, legal, and basic living services to battered women and their children since 1980. Families are eligible for these specific services if they are in imminent physical danger and have no access to other resources. These families have few, if any, emotional supports and come to the Safe Home as their only alternative. According to funding regulations, they are entitled to remain in residence for a maximum of 90 days.

Initially, the Safe Home focused therapeutic attention on the needs of the battered women. Over a period of time, staff came to realize that the children who had witnessed domestic violence also presented their own distressing symptoms. This observation was simultaneously substantiated in the professional literature (Levine, 1975; Moore, 1975; Rosenbaum and O'Leary, 1981). Among the children's symptoms were depression, excessive separation anxiety, psychosomatic concerns, low self-esteem, and feelings of powerlessness.

Through a grant from the New York State Department of Social Services in 1982, a Children's Project was established in the Safe Home with the goal of providing services directly and specifically to the youngsters. Included in the help given to the children was, and continues to be, the use of art as a significant medium for communication and self-expression. The artwork also provides a major vehicle by which the staff assesses each child's cognitive and emotional functioning.

In the course of the first two years of the Children's Service Project, clinical observations at the Safe Home demonstrated that many of the male children, some as young as three, were already incorporating the aggressive behavior witnessed in their fathers into their own actions and play. The female children, likewise viewing the spousal violence as "normal," were identifying with the victim role. The following vignette underscores this point:

> Two three-year-olds were playing in the living room together. The little boy, Dominic, asked the little girl, Lydia, "Can I kiss you?" She said, "No, we have to get married first." They danced around the living room and pretended to marry. Dominic then said, "Now?" Lydia replied, "No, we have to have a baby." Dominic ran and got a doll and they pretended it was their baby. Dominic anxiously asked again, "Can I kiss you?", to which Lydia replied, "You have to hit me first." Dominic obliged.

Another problem, observed frequently in children with younger siblings, has been their tendency to assume the mothering role for their sisters and brothers, and even for their mothers. This responsibility, which places incredible stress on the older sibling, eventually renders the child helpless and unable to cope as the demands progressively outweigh his or her abilities. For example, three-year-old Carey, who was living at the Safe Home, frantically attempted to feed and diaper her sisters, ages two years and 15 months, respectively. At the same time her mother, flipping through newspaper ads for apartment rentals, would ask her youngster's advice about where to live.

In almost every family that stays at the Safe Home there is a history of excessive family moves. These relocations, coupled with domestic violence, often lead to social isolation for the children. This, in turn, creates poor socialization skills, which are clearly demonstrated at the Safe Home both by the children's lack of "know how" in reaching out to other youngsters and by their inability to engage in cooperative play.

Infants who stay at the Safe Home almost universally have exhibited signs of the "failure to thrive" syndrome prior to admis-

4

sion. They are often underweight, depressed, and frequently ill. Once removed from the violent environment and relocated in the Safe Home, these young children show marked physical improvement. One 15-month-old, who had no teeth, grew three teeth during her brief stay. Another 36-month-old's chronic respiratory problem spontaneously improved.

The recurrent and cyclical effects of family violence upon successive generations, which have been suggested in the literature, have been substantiated by family histories of the women who stay at the Safe Home. In virtually every case, the husband had been an abused child, or witnessed the abuse of his mother, or both. The wives' family histories also reflect these factors in significant numbers, although not as frequently as those of the husbands'.

Unfortunately, the violence between the spouses also extends to the children in the Safe Home in at least 50 percent of the cases. It may take the form of direct physical abuse, incest, or the disguised form of "rough" play, such as six-year-old Kay described: "Every time I play with Daddy, I run away crying because it hurts when he pulls my hair and punches me."

These few examples illustrate how the pervasively destructive family relationships found in homes of domestic violence affect even the youngest of children. Sadly, as can be seen through this book, the effects continue to multiply and escalate as the child grows and develops.

Silent Screams and Hidden Cries presents the artwork of elementary-school-age children who have stayed at the Safe Home. While we collected a substantial representation from preschoolers, we felt it would be extremely difficult for the average untrained person to adequately understand the significance of the scribbles and symbols. The work of older children was not included because the sample was not large enough to be significant. The selection from elementary-school-age children, however, included a wide variety of artwork by youngsters of various socioeconomic backgrounds; it is particularly important because it can serve as a guide to professionals who have daily contact with children from the ages of five to 12 (see Appendix A).

The artwork included in this book was produced in a two-year period during which 47 children, ages five through 12, were in residence at the Safe Home. Of this number, many youngsters remained for less than one week and were not able to participate in the drawings necessary for inclusion in this book. However, artwork of five other children who did create drawings of houses, trees, persons, and families was excluded because their mothers refused to give the necessary parental consent. It is important to state that their drawings, too, projected the marked disturbances that will be noted throughout this book.

A large output of artwork by children of elementary school age is not surprising since this is the time in life when a child gains recognition through his or her productivity (Erickson, 1963). In fact, Freud (1938) acknowledged the productivity of this age, which he called the latency period. Freud described this stage of development as one in which physical drives are repressed and energies are rechanneled into socially approved activities. It is well known that art is a common vehicle for the release and expression of these energies.

Clinical observations at the Safe Home suggest a strong correlation between domestic violence and the disturbances in the development of the children's emotional and intellectual functioning. By identifying these disturbances through the youngsters' artwork, we hope to continue to sensitize lay persons and professionals to the profound effect of domestic violence on the child. In this way, the value of early intervention can be more adequately perceived and, hopefully, the cyclical effects of family violence can be broken.

We hope that *Silent Screams and Hidden Cries* will serve as an aid for social workers, psychologists, art therapists, teachers, and other professionals who work closely with children to help them recognize significant emotional disturbances and liabilities through the children's artwork. We trust these individuals will then make the necessary and appropriate referrals to prevent the development of further disabilities and to help the child to realize his or her maximum potential.

Children's Drawings: An Overview

As in any other skill or ability, drawing follows a developmental sequence. Rouma (as cited by Harris, 1963) conducted an extensive research project in which he studied children's abilities to draw, and he identified specific stages. The children initially develop an ability to hold, control, and manipulate the pencil. The youngster then works towards giving definition to scribbles and next moves on to plan what is going to be drawn. The forms progress and eventually resemble the objects the child intends to represent.

6

Harris (1963) cites Burt (1921) as also identifying specific steps in the progression of drawing. The *scribble*, which is generally produced from ages two to three years, involves non-goal-directed pencillings in which the major purpose is motor expression. This progresses into purposeful pencillings that become the major objective. The *scribble* moves on to *modeling*, based on adults' motions, which culminates in *localized scribbling*, in which the child attempts to draw parts of a specific concept.

At approximately age four the child produces *lines*. These are single motions in which parts of a person are randomly and sometimes disconnectedly placed. Burt labeled the next stage of drawing, in which body parts of the person become distinguishable, *descriptive symbolism*. This occurs around ages five to six.

The next age group (seven to nine or 10) draws a more true-to-life figure and adds more detail, such as clothing and decorations. The last phase that we will discuss for the purposes of this book is *visual realism*, which covers ages from 10 to approximately 11. The major progression here is related to an improvement of technical skills. This is mainly accomplished through reproducing the work of others. Two-dimensional and three-dimensional drawing is more common at this age.

With this brief analysis of the developmental stages involved in drawing, we would like to move on to the content of the drawings produced by children that helps us to understand the child's inner world. When a child draws or paints, a graphic representation of the youngster's inner world is visually projected for us to view. Although each child's perception and representation are distinctly unique, a great deal of research in the fields of art therapy, psychology, and psychiatry has resulted in the development of specific methods for interpreting this artwork.

Specifically, projective drawings are useful in gathering information about an individual's cognitive and developmental levels, degree of flexibility, and overall personality integration. In addition, the quality of the child's interaction with the environment is graphically presented (Buck, 1981).

The manner in which a youngster approaches a drawing can be extremely revealing in terms of personality dynamics. The child may be happy or sullen, talkative or quiet, anxious or relaxed, self-confident or self-doubtful, dependent or independent (Hammer, 1980).

One should bear in mind that most children are not particularly artistically inclined nor talented, as Hammer has noted in his introduction to this book. Individuals learning to analyze projective drawings are often focused on whether skill or fluency in drawing influences the quality or scope of the interpretive material. That this is not so can be easily demonstrated by examining the art of such painters as Picasso, da Vinci, and Rembrandt. One needs only to look at their works to immediately recognize strong personality differences (Ogdon, 1981) (although omissions or emphases in their paintings are conscious decisions made often for aesthetic reasons).

A relatively healthy, well-integrated individual includes the important details of the object when drawing it. For a child, assessment of appropriate inclusions must be based on the youngster's chronological age, for which developmental norms have been carefully researched and established (Goodenough, 1926; Koppitz, 1968). Bear in mind that no single sign can be considered conclusive; rather, it is the totality of symbols that must be assessed.

A full battery of projective drawings often includes the House, Tree, Person, and Kinetic Family Drawing. While the drawings are being produced, the examiner takes notes on the sequence of detail, tempo, spontaneous comment, and general behavior. Upon completion of the drawing phase, a planned interview, or the Post-Drawing Interrogation, is initiated. This is a standardized set of questions that provide insights into various aspects of the drawings by having the children describe, clarify, and interpret the objects. It also allows the child to free associate and thereby provides the examiner an opportunity to increase his or her knowledge of the youngster.

Hammer (1980) discussed analyzing the content of the artwork. Such aspects as the postural tone of the figures, the emphasis upon various individual aspects, or the facial expression all combine to give the interpreter valuable information. Hammer and others speak to the importance of observing the sequence, as parts of the drawings emerge. Drive derivatives, defenses, and adaptation of the individual can be gauged and reflected by the stages of each drawing's development, and the drawings provide a series of recorded behavior samples. In addition, sequences for houses, trees, and persons have been established to help interpret the artist's emerging picture.

The size of the image presented on the paper is highly significant (Buck, 1981; Di Leo, 1973; Hammer, 1980; Jolles, 1971; Ogdon, 1981) and provides a measure of the subject's self-esteem. An average human figure, for instance, drawn by a child on an

8½"×11" piece of paper should be under nine inches (Koppitz, 1968; Ogdon, 1981). If a drawing is larger, this may indicate personality features such as aggression, grandiosity, and compensatory defenses (Ogdon, 1981). Conversely, if we are presented with a tiny drawing, this may infer inadequacy, inferiority, low self-esteem, anxiety, depression, and a weak ego (Hammer, 1980; Ogdon, 1981).

Detailing is another aspect that is examined in drawing interpretation. This feature mirrors an individual's awareness and interest in the outside world (Jolles, 1971). Hammer (1980) believes that inadequate detail suggests an inner emptiness, a low energy level, depression, and an introversive type of personality. Ogdon (1981), in his review of the literature, has found that excessive use of detail represents an abnormally strong need to structure the total environment. Jolles further states that an analysis of the type of details included facilitates a better understanding of the specific conflict represented. As noted earlier, the type and amount of details that, according to established norms, are expected to be present in a drawing are commensurate with the age of the artist (Harris, 1963; Koppitz, 1968).

Erasures in the production must also be considered in the analysis of a drawing. When erasures are used in moderation and followed by improvement in the drawing, this indicates a flexibility and an ability to be critical of one's own work (Ogdon, 1981). However, when excessive erasures are noted, uncertainty, indecisiveness, and generalized dissatisfactions with oneself are suggested (Hammer, 1980; Ogdon, 1981). Jolles (1971) adds that if the production deteriorates in redrawing, then a conflict may exist regarding either the object or what it symbolically represents.

Placement of the figure or object is also an important factor for consideration. A central placement of the drawn work is normal and suggests that the person is reasonably secure (Ogdon, 1981). Hammer (1980) adds that this indicates that the individual is self-directed and self-centered. An image placed above the midline suggests that there are strong strivings towards goals that are unrealistic; it may also reveal that fantasy is largely utilized as a mechanism for coping (Jolles, 1965; Ogdon, 1981). A rendering placed below the midline may be interpreted as the artist's feelings of insecurity, depression, reality-boundedness, and concreteness in thinking (Hammer, 1980; Jolles, 1964; Ogdon, 1981).

The side of the page that is utilized is significant, as it also projects attitudes in regard to the self. Placement on the right

9

side, according to Ogdon (1981), suggests a degree of intellectualizing, control, and behavior that is largely governed by the "reality principle." This may also suggest that the person is preoccupied with concerns about the future (Jolles, 1971). Objects on the left side of the page have been thought to reflect a more impulsive individual who is focused on the past (Jolles, 1971; Ogdon, 1981).

The pressure exerted by the pencil may also be revealing. When it is fairly consistent throughout the drawn work, this implies that the artist is "normal" and "stable" (Ogdon, 1981). It may also be a gauge of the individual's energy level (Hammer, 1980). Heavy strokes suggest inner tension, forcefulness, and a tendency to act aggressively (Hammer, 1980; Ogdon, 1981), while light pencillings project a personality that is colored by hesitation, fearfulness, and indecisiveness (Di Leo, 1983; Hammer, 1980; Machover, 1980).

The treatment of lines is also of particular note. The quality of the strokes is examined, considering such factors as firmness, straightness, length, sketchiness, rigidity, and curvature. For example, a firm stroke may indicate that when the artist approaches a task he or she is determined, persistent, and secure. Conversely a sketchy line may reflect one who is uncertain, shy, and insecure (Ogdon, 1981).

Other aspects that are essential to review in a full drawing analysis are transparencies, symmetrics, omissions, distortions, proportions, shading, and weather. A number of fine books are available for a more in-depth analysis of children's artwork and are listed at the end of this book.

In *Silent Screams and Hidden Cries*, we will be examining examples of Human Figure Drawings, Kinetic Family Drawings, houses, and trees. The interpretations which will be presented are not intended to represent the only possible analyses of these drawings, nor will they be all-inclusive. Rather, they will highlight specific areas of each drawing that we feel will help the reader to better understand and appreciate the artwork. It is our hope that through these illustrations, the reader will also gain knowledge about the devastating, sometimes catastrophic effects on children who live in homes where they are witnesses to domestic violence.

CHAPTER 2

THE HUMAN FIGURE DRAWING

Overview

Of all the types of drawings created by children, the human figure is the favorite subject (Griffith, 1935) and is also closest to being the child's inner self-portrait. According to Hammer (1980), drawing a person can elicit a youngster's feelings about the self, the ideal self, and perceptions of significant individuals in his or her life, such as a mother, father, sister, or brother. In addition, a child's personality traits, attitudes, concerns, and interpersonal skills are represented through this vehicle.

The Human Figure Drawing (HFD) is used extensively, as are drawings of the house, tree, and family, as a projective test by trained psychotherapists. This method of personality analysis is based on carefully developed and validated interpretations by such notables in the field as Machover (1980), Hammer (1980), Di Leo (1983), Jolles (1971), and others. When used in this way, the child is given instructions to "draw a person." Generally, the drawing is created in pencil and may be followed by a crayon drawing. Koppitz (1968) states that the pictorial response to the task of creating a Human Figure Drawing represents a graphic form of communication between the child and the therapist and, as such, differs from spontaneous drawings children may make when they are alone or with friends.

When analyzing the Human Figure Drawing, the examiner/therapist studies the drawing, noting the general themes of size, placement, line quality and pressure, spontaneity or rigidity, and the emotions it elicits, such as sadness, joy, or isolation. Attention is then paid to the inclusion and omission of numerous specifics, such as the head, facial features, body and body parts, limbs, hands, fingers, clothing, and the presence of extraneous details, such as clouds or another person. Reference to substantive studies is invaluable in understanding the significance of the many details. The work by Koppitz (1968) has particular relevance in analyzing children's Human Figure Drawings.

In her book, *Psychological Evaluation of Children's Human Figure Drawings*, Koppitz (1968) identifies 30 indicators of potential emotional disturbances. These indicators, derived from her own clinical experience, as well as the work of Machover and Hammer, include three types of items. The first is that which relates to the quality of the drawing, such as poor integration of parts of the figure, shading of the face or part of it, shading of the body and/or limbs, hands and/or neck, gross asymmetry of limbs, tiny figures of less than two inches, and large figures of more than nine inches. The second category consists of items or features not usually found in Human Figure Drawings, such as crossed eyes, teeth, arms too short to reach the waistline, arms that reach below the knees, hands as big as the face, arms without hands and/or fingers, legs pressed together, genitals, and the presence of rain or snow.

Like the factors delineated above, the following omissions (which would be expected in Human Figure Drawings of children at specific ages), comprise the third category of items included in Koppitz's list of potential emotional indicators: eyes, nose, mouth, body, and arms (should be included once boys are six and girls are five); feet (expected from boys by age nine and girls by age seven); neck (should be present by age 10 for boys and age nine for girls).

Koppitz strongly emphasizes that a number of these emotional indicators must be present to signal the potential for emotional disturbance and, as stated before, some factors must be examined with respect to the artist's age, since their presence may, in fact, be common until a certain age. An example of this is a Human Figure Drawing that is nine inches or more in height. This size person frequently occurs in HFDs of young children, and, as such, its presence cannot be considered clinically significant until a youngster is eight years old.

Koppitz (1968) has also developed a list of Normative Data for 30 Developmental Items found in the Human Figure Drawing.

These are details that typically appear only in a few HFDs of younger age children and increase in frequency of occurrence as the children grow older. While the head, body, and legs are generally present on the HFDs of children by age five, other items, such as arms, shoulders, pupils, mouth, and fingers, continue to increase in frequency of occurrence from ages five to 12. Significantly, Koppitz's research reveals that the frequency of the occurrence of most of the developmental items is not affected by the children's drawing ability.

Importantly, the Human Figure Drawing can also be used to assess a child's intellectual or conceptual development and/or neurological impairment. The Goodenough and Harris Drawing Test score (Harris, 1963) has shown a strong correlation with I.Q. scores in intelligence tests, such as the WISC-R, for children between the ages of five and 10. Their system provides a methodology for measuring 78 details of the HFD.

The Human Figure Drawings presented on the following pages were administered as projective tests and were usually drawn in pencil. The information that we will share with you, however, will offer some generalized themes that may be applicable to children's spontaneous drawings as well. We wish to caution you, the reader, that no single projective drawing, regardless of how carefully it may be administered or analyzed, should ever be viewed as a definitive measure of the child's emotional or cognitive development. Rather, a full battery of drawings must be administered and assessed with consideration given to the youngster's developmental and family history, his or her current life situation, and other available data.

Kay

Person 1

Five-year-old Kay is the older of two siblings. Her younger brother is three years old. Kay has moved five times in the last five years. The entire family has lived intermittently with the paternal extended family, in which violence has been pervasive. While Kay has not been physically abused herself, she has witnessed her father beating her mother and her uncles. He has also been frequently arrested and jailed for the physical assault and battery of strangers. The spouse abuse, which has been chronic for the past 10 years, finally culminated in the mother's and children's admittance into the Safe Home. The last episode involved the husband grabbing his wife by the throat and screaming, "I'm going to kick your stinkin' face in." Throwing her on the ground, he proceeded to do just that. Kay's mother called her daughter into the room, anticipating that this five-year-old could come to her defense. In fact, the father did stop his attack once Kay was present.

We are struck with the grotesque quality of Kay's figure, mirroring the horror of her life experiences. The arms cannot be used to reach, hold, or touch. Rather, they appear to be clubs used for defense. Further confirmation of her defensive stance is found in the enlarged, rounded teeth. However, one senses her helplessness in the lack of secure attachment of either the arms or the blunted teeth.

Di Leo (1973) states that the shaded parts of the human figure have repeatedly been observed in drawings by anxious children. The intensity of the shading in Kay's drawing is indicative of her excessive anxiety regarding her genital area and may indicate her concerns about sexual abuse. The shading of the legs, which are vehicles for mobility, confirms her inability to move away from her powerless situation. The eyes in this figure are significant: grotesque in their terrified quality. In addition, the pupils move in divergent directions. We sense that this child is so frightened by what she sees that she cannot bear to focus. We see reflected in this drawing a child whose development has been severely disturbed.

Andrew
Person 2

Six-year-old Andrew, the oldest of three children, should have been able to include the body and arms in his Human Figure Drawing, according to the developmental norms for his age. The omission of the upper limbs reveals his inability to manipulate and control his environment in a manner appropriate for his age. The omissions of the body and the arms are not surprising. In fact, these symbols reflect Andrew's reaction to living with an alcoholic, unemployed father who physically and verbally assaulted his wife from the beginning of their marriage, and, later, did the same to their younger children. The abuse to the wife continued throughout all three of her pregnancies and involved continuous hitting, punching, shoving, verbal assaults, and even threats at knifepoint. The last episode was particularly terrifying to Andrew's mother, since his father had been arrested and sentenced for stabbing a passerby.

As stated earlier Koppitz (1968), who has developed Normative Data for Developmental Items on Human Figure Drawings for boys and girls from five to 12 years old, relates that the absence of both the body and the arms in the drawings of a six-year-old boy reflects developmental arrest. Psychological testing has confirmed that Andrew has not been able to achieve the normal level of intellectual development for his age.

Looking further at the drawing, we are struck by the confusion of body parts. Are the ears, in fact, ears, or attempts at arms? Does the circle between the eyes represent the nose, or is the nose represented by the line above the mouth? When Andrew was asked what the shaded circle below the mouth was, he was unable to answer.

This confusion parallels Andrew's life experiences. During his six years of life, he has been uprooted from his home, friends, and family countless times, the last of which was his short stay at the Safe Home. He remained there for only two weeks, after which time his mother returned, with Andrew, to her husband.

Carol

Person 3

The most striking aspect of this figure, drawn by Carol, age five, is its size. Di Leo (1983) has written that insecure, anxious children tend to draw small figures that timidly occupy only a small area of the available space. In addition, Buck (1981) states that a tiny figure represents feelings of inadequacy and a tendency to withdraw from the environment. The placement of Carol's figure on the extreme left alerts us to her overconcern with herself and her past. The lack of feet in the drawing further confirms her sense of helplessness and "lack of sure footing." All these points have been validated by clinical observations of this shy, isolated, and nonassertive child. While Carol has not been a direct victim of abuse, she has nonetheless been victimized by seeing rampant violence around her.

The abuse of Carol's mother began in adolescence, while she was dating her future husband. He was then, and still is, an alcohol and drug abuser. He would beat her, rape her, and then laugh at her. At other times, he forced her to have sex with his brother. Following Carol's conception, her father was sentenced to a two-year prison term for sodomizing an adolescent girl. He is currently awaiting trial for rape. During the family's stay at the Safe Home, the mother confided that she felt lost and helpless. We see these same feelings mirrored in Carol's figure, which may, in fact, represent her identification with her mother.

Ned

Person 4

Ned, age six, is the older brother of Carol, who drew Person 3. A
similar feeling of helplessness is also present in his drawing. In
addition, we can't help but notice the intense shading on the left
side of the page. This indicates anxiety over the past and echoes his
sister's similar concern, as shown in Person 3. We sense that this
boy feels cornered and powerless in his environment.

Because Ned has chosen to reduce the space that is accessible to
him on the paper, it appears that he has already begun to view his
environment as seriously limiting in what it can offer him. He may
actively constrict the environmental stimulation as a way of coping
with life. As an example, we have noticed that in his interactions
with his mother and sister at the Safe Home he "pulls out of the
picture." This was literally demonstrated when the two children and
mother were asked to draw a picture together. Ned stayed by
himself and, drawing on a small section of the page, sketched a boy
crying. His mother and sister actively created a fantasy world of
flowers, a house, and a lake.

We see from Persons 3 and 4 that both Ned and Carol are experiencing such discomfort that they are individually developing
ways of surviving which portend a difficult future for each child.

Lorraine

Person 5

Looking at this drawing, one senses that the person depicted is either being crucified or pinned down. Six-year-old Lorraine has spent all the years of her young life witnessing the episodic, severe beatings her father has inflicted on her mother. Lorraine's father began abusing her mother within the first year of their marriage. He has punched her in the head and chest, choked her with his hands, her bra, and her stockings, shoved her, and even shot at her with a rifle. He is an active alcoholic who drinks several bottles of vodka daily. Lorraine's way of coping with this environment has been to hide in a closet, whimpering.

The absence of well-defined hands and feet in this drawing sensitizes us to Lorraine's helplessness. In addition, she not only lacks "a foot to stand on," but also cannot control or manipulate her environment.

Lorraine does include breasts and possibly a vagina on this figure. She also places great emphasis on the neck, and even includes a necklace on this otherwise naked body. The neck, which separates the head from the body, is regarded as the connection between intellectual control and bodily drives. Hammer (1980) believes that beginning at age eight, the child becomes acutely aware of a need for power over his or her body, and therefore begins to draw a neck. The exceptionally long neck in this drawing alerts us to an area of difficulty for Lorraine. She strains to maintain control over her bodily concerns, impulses, and anxieties. In addition, play therapy sessions with her revealed incidents in which she had been sexually abused by her father. Although Lorraine is only six, the figure's elongated neck, the presence of the breasts, the phallic banana standing erect next to the figure, and the broken phallic-like left leg all indicate her premature sexual preoccupation and concern.

Another noteworthy point is the large size of the person in the drawing. This aspect of the figure is less subject to conscious control than others (Machover, 1980). Both the large amount of space used for the drawing and the "paper-chopping" (Jolles, 1971) on the top of the page suggest Lorraine's attempt to overcompensate for feelings of powerlessness. Likewise, the smile is her attempt to say, "It's OK." Yet, we notice that even this is not "holding up" well for it is rather crooked and stiff, much like having a "stiff upper lip." We wonder what would happen if Lorraine relaxed her rigid posture and defenses. Would she then curl up whimpering again?

Willy

Person 6

   Willy, the five-year-old brother of Lorraine (Person 5), has also shared the pervasive experience of continual domestic violence. We see in his drawing a pathetic, insect-like creature. Neither the disconnected wings nor the exaggerated teeth can help protect him. The wings cannot carry him away; the teeth, broken at the base, are weak and cannot defend him. This child, helplessly peeking out of tiny pupils, presents a fragmented identity.

   The framentation, distortion, and grotesque quality of this drawing indicate neurological impairment and, clearly, this drawing portrays a child whose development is pathological.

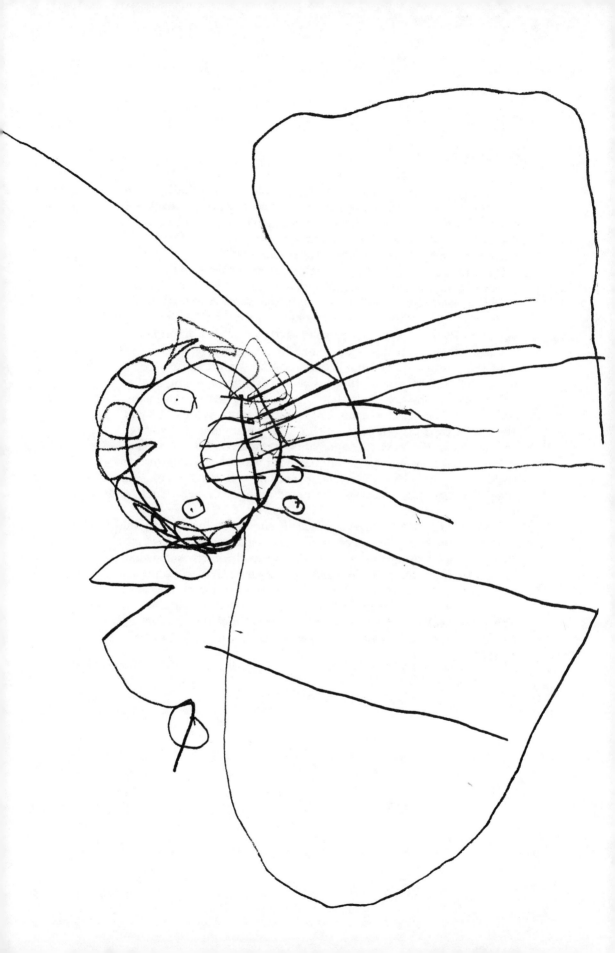

Pat

Person 7

Pat, age nine, came to the Safe Home after witnessing her father
drag her mother, in caveman fashion by her long hair, down three
flights of stairs. This was not the first episode of abuse Pat had
watched. As with the other children already presented, family
violence had been her constant companion.

Upon first glance, the figure in this drawing seems to be that of
a sweet young girl, much as Pat appears to be in life. Closer observation reveals intense shading and size constriction of the chest.
Since the chest is thought of as the holding tank for feelings, we are
alerted to Pat's tendency to cover up and restrict her emotions.

The inadequacy of the figure's arms is also striking. The figure's
right arm, intense in line quality, is not only significantly short but
also detached from the shoulder. The left arm, light in line quality
and constricted by the pocketbook, gives the appearance of being
mechanical. The helpless arms, rigid and lacking any flexibility at
the elbow (Koppitz, 1968, states that it is not unusual to see the
presence of an elbow at this age), appear unbalanced in both size
and line quality, echoing Pat's unbalanced way of reaching into the
world for support. Moreover, the absence of well-defined hands and
fingers further substantiates her limited ability to reach, touch, and
receive nurturance.

Another important element to note is the heavy line quality and
shading of the belt. This piece of clothing separates the constricted
chest, where no suggestion of breasts appear, from the somewhat
flared and decorated skirt. According to Jolles (1978), a heavily
shaded belt represents a conflict between the expression and the
control of sexuality. Since Pat's two older half-sisters had been
raped repeatedly by Pat's father, the projection of this conflict onto
the Human Figure Drawing is understandable and, sadly, to be
expected.

Jessica

Person 8

The enchanting little boy represented in Person 8 was drawn by Jessica, age 11, in response to the therapist's request to draw a figure of the opposite sex. Jessica had seen her stepfather punch and choke her mother with regularity. In addition, for the past five years he had sexually abused Jessica by fondling her genitals and by exposing his penis and encouraging her to stroke it. The abuse experienced by this family had been in the nature of both active assaults and active neglect. Although her stepfather earned a substantial living in his own construction company, his alcoholism "drank up" all of his funds. As a result, the family has suffered frequent evictions and has often been without food.

Hammer (1980) states that one of the possible subjects represented by a child's drawing may be that of a parental figure. In addition, the perception of the mother or father that the child reveals in the drawing frequently predicts personality traits that will later be incorporated by the child.

This drawing may very well portray Jessica's image of the father figure. Although this particular male figure is enticing and evokes a sense of helplessness, the image may represent the unconscious process by which Jessica is internalizing her perceptions of her stepfather's personality and character. The internalized image may be evolving into her generalized view of men. Jessica's stepfather had exhibited his helplessness in controlling his sexual impulses with her. Through his alcohol abuse and financial difficulties, he had also shown his inability to adequately care for himself and his family. As a result, it appears as if she has begun to see him, as well as other men, as being helpless and childlike. In Jessica's person drawing, we see short, stub-like arms ending in hands with undefined fingers. Since they are unable to reach out to others, the arms seem to be ineffectually pleading, "Take care of me; take care of me!"

Considering Jessica's life history, the transparent hat, through which the hair is seen, is particularly significant. As Machover (1980) has stated, this is indicative of primitive sexual behavior, and in this case we believe it reflects the father figure's primitive sexual behavior. Based on the interpretation that this drawing represents Jessica's internalized image of the father figure, a graphic communication of Jessica's evolving view of men is projected. We must note that the figure's eyes are closed and the mouth is smiling. It may be that she sees the father figure as one who cannot look at his own actions or his world, and we might also surmise that this view is one that Jessica herself cannot bear to see.

Harriet

Person 9

This figure, drawn by eight-year-old Harriet, gives the global impression of a frail, gentle, shy child. The feelings elicited in the viewer are those of wanting to envelop and protect this young girl. The tiny eyes, nose, and diminutive mouth, the short and tenuously attached arms, and the narrow and elongated legs combine to create a sense of her vulnerability.

Harriet's mother, Dianne, and father, Elmer, separated one year ago. Despite court orders commanding that he leave the home and not harass Dianne or their three daughters and son, Elmer continues to terrorize them. He often breaks into the home in the evening while the family is sleeping, surreptitiously enters Dianne's room and proceeds to stare at her until she awakens. He has also combed the neighborhood for her, packing a pistol and threatening to kill her. The repetition of these activities culminated in the family's entry into the Safe Home.

This drawing by Harriet mirrors the way she appears to the world. Her therapist at the Safe Home describes Harriet as "a quiet child, nonintrusive; one who watches and sees but does not say." This style of interaction reflects this youngster's way of coping with life. Thus far, it has served her well. Adults find her engaging and easy to love. This serves to counterbalance the lack of familial nurturance, helping Harriet to get what she needs in the way of adult protection, attention, and affection.

Brian

Person 10

Ten-year-old Brian was the first child born to 28-year-old Anna and 30-year-old John. The couple had attempted conception for eight years and was finally successful after medical intervention. However, after five months of caring for Brian, John and Anna found him too demanding a child to cope with and sent him south to his maternal grandmother's. Both parents were working full time, John during the day as a chemical worker, and Anna at night as a nurse's aide. When Brian came back home after three months, this work pattern continued.

At four years of age, two significant changes occurred in Brian's life — the birth of his brother, James, and the start of his father's verbal abuse towards his mother. During the next six years, John became increasingly aggressive in his threats to and verbal assaults on Anna and in his capacity for violence.

The family's eventual admission to the Safe Home was precipitated by John's purchase of a switch blade, his thrusting it into the wall, and his concurrent report to Anna that the walls were telling him to kill her. Brian and James's response to this nightmare was their development of a joint scheme to kill their father. This plan was overheard by Anna and so jolted her to the horrendous effects the father's behavior was having on the boys that she decided to leave the marital residence. Anna spoke repeatedly in the Safe Home about the devastating experience of leaving a house for which she had worked and saved for 18 years to then face existence in a one-bedroom apartment.

We see in Brian's drawing a well-defended and controlled boy. The figure is upright and seems to be at attention. Closer inspection, however, reveals several significant factors. Brian first began to draw a person on the lower half of the page. After five minutes of unsuccessful attempts to correct his drawing, he chose to begin again. The erasures of the original drawing, however, express Brian's anxiety and represent his need to alter and perfect (Machover, 1980). The shoulders appear flattened, almost as if the weight of what he has been carrying is too much to bear. The erasures show that Brian is unable to accept this view of himself but cannot adequately defend against it. This is manifested by the

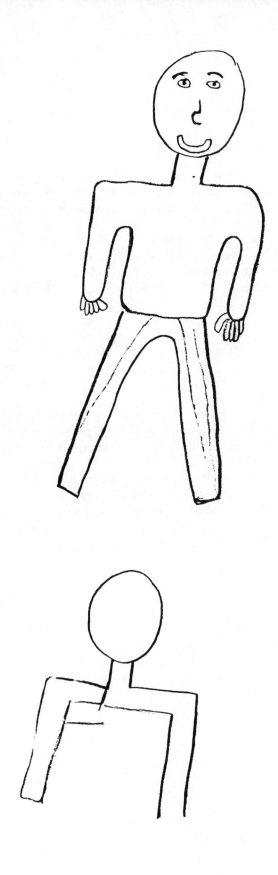

original incomplete figure and the boy's decision to begin a new drawing on the same page.

In the upper drawing, the figure's left shoulder is rounder and less rigid than the right shoulder, reflecting Brian's hope for a more manageable future. This hopefulness is further confirmed by the difference between the figure's left and right hands. The right-hand fingers are petal-like and, as such, represent a fragile and infantile form of negotiating the environment. The left hand is more maturely developed and portends a firmer grasp of what the future holds. Buck (1981), Jolles (1971), and Hammer (1980) would contend that the location of a figure's placement on the page reflects preoccupation with either the past (left side of the page) or the future (right side of the page). It is the authors' hypothesis that this concept can also be applied to the differential treatment of body parts between the left and the right sides of the body. Hence, we believe that the more developed left hand projects Brian's intent to struggle and gain mastery of his environment. At present, however, the absence of the figure's feet reflect Brian's current lack of ability to propel and direct himself in the world.

Two other noteworthy omissions in the drawing are the absence of the hair and ears. Koppitz (1968) states that 98 percent of the Human Figure Drawings created by 10-year-olds include hair, the traditional symbol of masculinity and strength. The baldheaded figure suggests that Brian is denying these qualities in himself. We believe this is because the male role model, as represented by his father, is not acceptable to the boy. This is further substantiated by the absence of the figure's ears. In this way, Brian protects and defends himself by not having to hear the abuse spewn by his father towards his mother.

James

Person 11

James, who is the six-year-old brother of Brian, presents us with a robot-type person. With its square body and spring-like neck we are reminded of the rigidity of Brian's person. However, this drawing represents a more disturbed child. According to Ogdon (1981), boxlike figures, drawn by children, are possible indicators of both emotional disturbances and acting-out tendencies.

The agitated lines that define and confine all of the person, with the exception of the head, tell us that James has a high anxiety level regarding his emotions and impulses. As stated earlier, the body is the seat of basic needs and drives (Jolles, 1971) and the chest has long been considered to be the container of one's feelings.

We note that the neck of the figure is heavily shaded and serves as a weak and fragile connection between the torso and the head. This further confirms the poor modulation between James's thoughts and feelings. This has been corroborated through his aggressive, acting-out behavior at the Safe Home.

The number of body parts present in this drawing is higher than average for James's age (Koppitz, 1968). According to Goodenough's scoring system (Goodenough, 1926), this suggests a mental age of seven years, nine months, clearly above that of his chronological age. It is apparent that James's intelligence is not in question. Rather, there are emotional factors that impede his functioning.

In this drawing, we again see a figure with no hair—no overt portrayal of virility. This mirrors Brian's baldheaded figure and alerts us to a possible danger signal to both boys' male identities.

Simon

Person 12

Ten-year-old Simon's superhero presents us with several immediate contradictions. While a heroic figure is generally the embodiment of strength, power, and control, this small superman, placed well above the midline of the page, belies these qualities. Koppitz (1968) reports that the typical height of a human figure, drawn on an 8½"×11" page, is approximately nine inches. Simon's two-inch figure, by virtue of its size, projects feelings of inferiority, ineffectiveness, inadequacy, and low self-esteem (Di Leo, 1973; Hammer, 1980). In addition, the placement of this drawing connotes that Simon aspires to goals that are beyond his ability to achieve (Jolles, 1971). Perhaps this is why he has chosen to represent himself through an image that is clearly an overcompensation for his inner feelings.

It is also no wonder that Simon is compelled to present a façade of strength. This is a boy who has repeatedly witnessed his mother being tied up and beaten by his stepfather. He himself has also been the victim of this man's brutality. In fact, most of Simon's body was scarred from lashings. This appalling situation was compounded by Simon's inability to reach out to his mother for assistance. He learned early that if he told her of the beatings he suffered, and she in turn confronted her husband, this man would retaliate by physically attacking her.

Another poignant contradiction in the drawing is the effeminate quality of this superhero. With short, curly hair, and a shirt that bears closer resemblance to a dress than a superhero's leotard, we see that Simon is unable to adequately integrate male identity. Perhaps being a strong man is too threatening and dangerous for this helpless 10-year-old boy.

Blanche

Person 13

This charming girl drawn by eight-year-old Blanche delights us on first viewing. However, the following story, told during the post-drawing interview, wipes the smile from our faces; and although the drawing itself has many significant aspects, in this discussion we will be addressing the relevance of Blanche's narrative. She related the following tale in response to the request to tell a story about the person in the drawing: "She had an accident and broke her two hands off. She was walking across the street alone and a drunk driver broke her hands. When she came out of the hospital she wanted some cereal, but she couldn't get any. Then she got some, and her mother fixed the rest. . . . "

The post-drawing interrogation provides the artist with an important opportunity to define, describe, modify, and elaborate upon the drawing through associations that are not necessarily conscious (Buck, 1981). The use of these associations also provides an invaluable method of indirect interview, which furnishes information that may not otherwise be accessible (Machover, 1980).

Blanche's story reveals her vulnerability resulting from the active negligence of others. In this tale, she loses her hands, is forced to struggle in order to take care of herself, and eventually receives assistance from her mother. In actual life, Blanche's natural father had a drinking problem that contributed to the termination of the marriage. Subsequently, her mother married another man who eventually began to abuse her. The abuse involved being repeatedly beaten with a stick on her legs, back, stomach, and face. After three years of enduring this maltreatment, her mother successfully left the marital residence by entering the Safe Home. The mother's ability to leave two unhealthy relationships attests to her inner resources and may account for the somewhat positive conclusion to Blanche's story, in which the child is able to receive assistance from her mother.

Dennis

Person 14

The excessive number of details presented in this Human Figure Drawing by 11-year-old Dennis is an unusual phenomenon. It indicates a high anxiety level, which he tries to control by superimposing structure (Jolles, 1971). The abundance of objects Dennis has drawn is his attempt to create a world in which he is master. Had Dennis created a single person, unencumbered by nonessential details, he may have felt more susceptible to forces beyond his control. By filling the space around himself as he stands behind the table, he attempts to defy outside influences.

Other indices of Dennis's anxiety are seen in this drawing as well. Koppitz (1968) found that clouds were drawn most often by very anxious children. The presence of the three spontaneously drawn clouds in this picture reveals that Dennis feels very threatened by the adult world (Koppitz, 1968), for he is literally standing under a cloud—in fact under three—and is under great pressure from above.

Another suggestion of Dennis's anxiety is contained in the treatment of the hair on both figures. The fragmented lines are intensely agitated and create a shaded effect. Jolles (1971) states that heavily shaded hair is an expression of anxiety. These three examples—the excessive number of details included in the drawing, the presence of clouds, and the shaded hair—are repeated expressions of Dennis's anxiety about himself and his relationship to the world.

An interesting aside is the symbolism projected by these clouds. The small enclosed window on the upper left of the picture might even be interpreted as a Kinetic Family Drawing (see Chapter 3). A parallel exists between the number of clouds presented here and the total number of members in Dennis's family—Dennis, his mother, and his father. We also observe that the two lower clouds are merged, while the third cloud, positioned above, appears to be drifting away from them. In fact, it seems to be moving towards the sun, and if its present course continues, the lone cloud will soon be blocking its rays. Clinical observation and psychological testing at the Safe Home have revealed that Dennis and his mother are involved in a symbiotic relationship. Since the sun is a symbol of warmth and love, we might conclude that this small drawing within the Human

Figure Drawing represents the separation of Dennis's father from his wife and son, and also his potential obstruction to their warmth and nurturance.

A final point about this Human Figure Drawing concerns the presence of the second person. This unusual aspect has not been seen in any of the other 75 drawings created by the children who resided at the Safe Home. Although Koppitz (1968), in the Draw-A-Person Test, does not list the addition of one other figure as an emotional indicator of pathology, given the clinical observation discussed above the authors believe it further confirms the unhealthy relationship between Dennis and his mother. It causes us to wonder if, without her in the picture, Dennis can feel complete.

Marilyn

Person 15

This girl, drawn jumping rope, is presented to us by Marilyn, age eight. Burns and Kaufman, in *Actions, Styles and Symbols in Kinetic Family Drawings* (1972), discuss eight drawings of children jumping rope. They conclude that this symbol may serve any or all of the following purposes: The rope encapsulates the child and protects the youngster from the environment; and it also focuses the viewer's attention.

We would like to invite you to imagine yourself as a child jumping rope and to feel what this activity evokes in you. You might feel yourself releasing energy and discharging anxiety. You might also be aware of the comforting repetition of your movements, and the solitary, almost isolating quality of this sport. If another person were to try to approach you while you were jumping, she or he would be either kept at a distance or hit by the rope.

The drawing of this activity may represent a sample of Marilyn's behavioral style. It is significant that the rope was added to this picture in the post-drawing interview, during which time Marilyn was asked to talk about the figure. Perhaps it was her way of telling the interviewer, "Stay away and don't touch me. You are getting too close."

Marilyn is an only child and, of necessity, has spent a great deal of time playing alone. Erikson talks about the role of play as preparation for adult life (Erikson, 1963). If this form of play, jumping rope, indeed represents a developing pattern for Marilyn, we are concerned about her evolving interpersonal skills.

A great deal of anxiety is revealed in this drawing. The excessive shading in the treatment of the hair (Ogdon, 1981), the repetition of the flowers on the dress, and the heavy line pressure throughout the figure (Hammer, 1980), all point to a high level of anxiety. The numerous erasures, which we see on the head, face, feet, hands, and legs, further confirm the intensity of this feeling. The site of an erasure, and/or the symbolic meaning attached to the particular site, points to a specific area of conflict for the artist. Marilyn erased and redrew almost every body part of this Human Figure Drawing,

thereby indicating conflict in many areas of her inner and outer worlds.

For all of Marilyn's eight years, she has witnessed her father abusing her mother. Her entry into the Safe Home was precipitated by a rageful encounter, in which her father violently expressed his fury over her mother's late return from a meeting at Marilyn's school. He slapped his wife so forcefully that her glasses flew off. He then twisted them, and commanded both the mother and child to leave the house.

Unfortunately, this marital experience mirrors the family interactions witnessed by Marilyn's parents in their own childhood. As discussed by Straus, Gelles, and Steinmetz (1981), and further confirmed by our own statistics, in which 72 percent of either the victims or the abusers were raised in violent homes, domestic violence certainly appears to breed domestic violence from generation to generation. Young Marilyn has viewed it repeatedly and the intense, watchful eyes in this drawing attest to her need to keep herself prepared and alert for the next explosion. Luckily, this figure also reveals that Marilyn is a bright child, able to reach out to others for assistance, with adequate legs and feet to enable her to move and stand up in the world.

CHAPTER 3

THE KINETIC
FAMILY DRAWING

Overview

Just as Gestalt psychologists concluded that the whole is greater than the sum of its parts, the family as a system is more powerful than the total of the individual members. The family is a dynamic interacting force, which influences the growth and development of the offspring and the continued evolution of the parents. The child's self-concept is intricately woven as the youngster slowly matures in the familial surroundings. In the process of growing, identification of the child's self evolves through the internalization of the parents' or parental figures' feelings and values. If these are positive and growth-enhancing, the offspring may develop healthy and positive self-concepts. If these feelings and values are negative, the youngsters may develop negative self-concepts. The family's history, dynamics, and value structure, therefore, mandate attention. A full appreciation of the child's personality cannot be understood without them.

When a child is told, "Draw your family doing something" (the Kinetic Family Drawing), the child's subjective family experience is graphically presented. Burns and Kaufman (1972) espouse the idea that the Kinetic Family Drawing (KFD) is a statement of how the child perceives himself or herself in the family setting and of how the youngster views the interactions between family members.

Historically, the child was simply asked to draw his or her family as part of a battery of projective tests. Burns and Kaufman, after two decades of testing in this format, further developed the technique by requesting that the youngster draw his or her family "doing something." They hypothesized that this additional information would shed light on the child's interpersonal relationships.

In his recent book, *Self-Growth in Families* (1982), Burns suggests that the following types of questions demonstrate the diversity of information available to the therapist when analyzing the Kinetic Family Drawing: What is your first impression? Whom and what do you see? What is happening? How do you feel about what is happening? Would you like to be a member of this family?

In interpreting children's Kinetic Family Drawings, specific points should also be noted. As in the production of the Human Figure Drawing, each person represented is individually evaluated. It is important to be cognizant of how the people in the Kinetic Family Drawing are using their bodies. For instance, are they using them to show off, hide, or be seductive? Do they seem proud or ashamed? The manner in which each person is drawn symbolizes how that family member is perceived by the child.

Satir (1967), in discussing the role of verbal and nonverbal communication in families, defines it as a means of interaction and transaction. She further states that the types of communication a person uses are reliable indices of his or her interpersonal functioning. The child's perception of the communication within the family is graphically depicted in the Kinetic Family Drawing by such factors as where the members are placed, both on the page and in relationship to each other, and the type and quality of activity in which the family is involved. For example, are the family members engaged in a tug-of-war, placed on opposite sides of the page from each other, or are they at a family picnic all actively cooking together?

Another factor relating to Satir's theory is the use of nonverbal messages as they are transmitted through body language. This is reflected in the Kinetic Family Drawing by the position, gesture, and stance of the figures. Is one person standing facing one or more family members? Does one person have his or her back turned to another? Is someone's arms folded tightly over his or her chest? Does one family member have his or her eyes closed?

Haley (1976), in *Problem Solving Therapy*, discusses family coalitions and alliances. He defines a coalition as a process of joined actions against a third person. An alliance differs in that two people share a common interest that is not shared by a third person. In the Kinetic Family Drawing, the child's perception of family alliances, coalitions, and family disharmonies is projected. If characteristically in the family one parent sides with the child against the other parent, then we might see a drawing in which the youngster and mother are on the left side of the page, and the father, removed from them, is placed on the right side. The post-drawing interview will also provide information further clarifying and defining the child's view of the family's coalitions and alliances.

In his book, *Family Therapy and Clinical Practice* (1978), Bowen talks about the continuum along which an individual differentiates himself or herself from the family. This theoretical line begins with an individual's total dependency and ends with his total differentiation. Bowen maintains that a healthy person would fall somewhere in the midpoint area. When family members are fused, and there is little sense of individuation, there is concern for the family's health. In a drawing this is reflected in the figures' similarities and differences. Are the figures all the same height regardless of the ages? Are they wearing the same clothes? Are they all in the same position or stance? It is important to realize that some similarities are to be expected. The alliance and identification of a son with his father may be shown by such repetitions as body posture and/or clothing. However, some differences, reflecting a separate sense of self, should also be present.

Minuchin (1981), in his theory of structural family therapy, addresses the issue of boundaries between the parents and children. The parents should be a separate entity with explicit roles of power and dominance. When the family system has broken down, a child may assume the responsibility or role of a parent. This is clearly depicted in the Kinetic Family Drawing by the size of the child in relation to the parent (when inconsistent with reality), and the child's role in the family activity portrayed. Is the child cooking dinner for the parents? Where the child is placed in relation to the ground line and the parents is also significant. Is the youngster standing above the parents, looking down on them?

Other factors to consider in analyzing the Kinetic Family Drawing are omissions of family members, including the artist, and erasures, which most often point to some type of conflict. In addition, Burns and Kaufman (1972) allude to the importance of the drawing style and suggest some questions of which to be mind-ful. Is there compartmentalization of the family members? Are they on different sides of the sheet of paper? Are barriers erected between family members? Who is taller, or shorter, in the draw-ing (again, if inconsistent with reality)? Who is placed in the foreground and who in the background?

The orientation of the father towards the artist (or self figure) and his direction towards the other persons in the drawing are of key importance. O'Brien and Patton (1974) studied the Kinetic Family Drawing and concluded that children who drew their fathers facing them scored higher on social and peer concepts than children who drew their fathers facing in a different direction.

The compilation of all these factors will be the foundation of rich data about the child's family that may not otherwise be ac-cessible to the practitioner.

Lynn

Family 1

Lynn, who is five years old, is the youngest sibling in a family that consists of her, two older sisters (ages 13 and 14), and her parents. Her mother has been married 18 years. Throughout this time, the mother has been continuously smacked in the face, thrown on the floor, and, in addition, hit by her husband with a telephone receiver against her head. She has suffered permanent hearing loss due to these assaults. Lynn's father is a retired New York City police sergeant, actively alcoholic, who had been hospitalized for detoxification five times over the past year alone. Lynn's mother told her therapist at the Safe Home, "I live in constant terror."

In Lynn's drawing of her family "doing something," we are struck by the floating, disconnected heads. Disproportionately large smiles fill faces that do not look at or relate to each other. Although the family ostensibly sits around a dinner table, as it was described by Lynn, there is no sense of a nurturing environment. Food is generally accepted as symbolic for being fed—both physically and emotionally. Yet Lynn drew the food with such heavy shading that the paper was torn. This clearly signals intense anxiety regarding the satisfaction of her needs through the family. This situation is exacerbated by the omission of arms and hands for all family members. This precludes any individual from being able to satisfy his or her own needs. It is important to point out that by age five, Lynn should be developmentally capable of producing arms and legs. The fact that no one family member is drawn with limbs reflects Lynn's perception of the family's inability to control and impact on its world, or to reach out and secure satisfaction from each other. In light of the other details included, such as eyelashes, noses, hair, eyes, and wide smiles, we also suspect that Lynn may be defending against her fear of assault. In contrast to the inclusion of all these other details, as long as there are no arms or hands to hit with or feet or legs to kick with, no one in the family can be hurt.

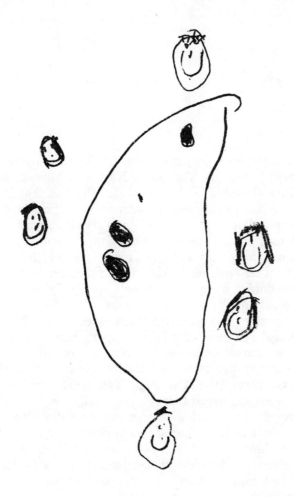

Kay

Family 2

As does her Human Figure Drawing (Person 1), these figures by five-year-old Kay again horrify us. The family Kay drew consists of her paternal "Grandma, Grandpa, and Aunt May." The fact that it does not include either Kay or the three other members of her immediate family is extremely significant. As Burns (1982) suggests, children may seek family substitutes when they cannot identify with their own nuclear family. Kay's family experiences, which involve witnessing her father beat her mother and uncles, are not positive or growth-producing images with which to identify. As a result, Kay unconsciously drew her family as consisting of her grandparents and aunt since she perceives these extended family members as her greatest source of emotional support. However, when we look at these figures, we do not feel very secure. The enlarged eyes, the sharp, spiked teeth, and the intense treatment of the hair all point to her perception of an angry and aggressive family. This has, in fact, been confirmed through the family history.

In the three figures drawn, the chaotic presence, as well as the absence, of arms, hands, and toes suggests inconsistency in the family's pattern of reaching out, holding, and nurturing Kay, and providing stability in her life. In addition, the large empty sockets of the eyes project the family members' reluctance to see what is happening. They are "blind" to the environment.

An important aspect of each Kinetic Family Drawing is the child's description and discussion of it. Such areas as what the family is doing, who is most happy, who is least happy, how the family members get along, and other relevant issues of family life provide essential information that is used in the analysis of family dynamics. In discussing what the family was doing, Kay stated, "They were busy raking leaves." Burns and Kaufman (1972) indicate that leaves are associated with dependency needs because they are originally attached to the nurturing source of the tree. Yet, in Kay's verbal description, the leaves are detached, paralleling the relationship of the family members to each other. Importantly, Kay has been detached from her grandparents and aunt through the marital separation and her stay at the Safe Home. Nothing connects the dead leaves to the tree in Kay's story, and we wonder if this may express Kay's helpless sense of familial security and her pessimistic view of her own future.

Carol and Ned

Families 3 and 4

Both families drawn by siblings Carol, age five, and Ned, age six, are noteworthy, in part because of the omissions of some family members. Carol, in Family 3 (see illustration below), drew a picture of her mother and father and stated, "The children are outside playing." Ned, on the other hand (Family 4), drew himself and his father standing alongside his dad's truck, going to see his mother (see illustration on facing page). Both drawings present such strong, though invisible, barriers between family members that excluded individuals are literally "not in the picture." Those that are included are unable to connect with each other because they do not have arms or hands. Since both Ned and Carol have demonstrated their abilities to draw arms and hands in their person drawings (Persons 3 and 4), the disconnectedness of the family in these pictures is underscored. In Carol's drawing of her parents, we see ghost-like figures, suggesting that she cannot touch or connect with them. The head of the mother (figure on the left, Family 3) is balanced

tenuously, reflecting the child's image that her mother's "head is not on straight" and that the mother is unstable. Ned's Human Figure Drawing (Person 4) suggests that he limits his environment as a way of coping. The father drawn by Carol (figure on right, Family 3) has only one pupil and therefore is unable to see the "whole picture." "To see or not to see," that is the question of the ambivalence. Here, we wonder if Carol also senses the father's similar coping style and therefore has drawn him with limited vision.

In the description of Person 4, we also discussed how Ned excluded himself when the mother and children drew a picture together. In Family 4, we see evidence that Ned identifies with his father by including only the two of them in his Kinetic Family Drawing, and by creating them in an almost identical fashion. We note that both figures have eyes but lack mouths, ears, noses, and arms. Through their limited sensing capacities, they can see but they cannot smell or hear, nor can they verbalize or touch. Moreover, they can react and respond only to the extent that they can use their legs and feet to move to and fro.

Ned regulates the interaction between his parents by leaving out his mother and sister. By so doing, he keeps the violence at a distance. This is confirmed further by the presence of a truck, which is needed to take Ned and his father to his mother. While Carol draws the parents together (Family 3) by excluding herself and Ned, she, likewise, is able to distance herself from the scene of the domestic violence.

Ellen

Family 5

Unlike the families previously presented, the domestic violence in Ellen's family has not been spouse abuse. Rather, Ellen's mother has been physically beaten with a cane by her own father for all of her 26 years. Ellen's parents were never married and, while the child has been in contact with her natural father, he lives more than a thousand miles away and is able to offer only limited emotional support. Ellen, age six, and her mother have always lived with her maternal grandparents and, upon discharge from the Safe Home, have successfully moved from that home for the first time. Leaving her parents had been an ongoing struggle for Ellen's mother. Each attempt to live independently was thwarted by Ellen's grandfather, who verbally and physically harassed the young mother into returning. With support and therapeutic intervention by the Safe Home staff, Ellen and her mother now have relocated to another state.

The immediate image projected by Ellen's Kinetic Family Drawing is that of a twisted and contorted group of individuals. The grandfather, on the extreme right, is portrayed partly as an animal. This is demonstrated by the gorilla-like arms and hoof-like hands and feet. The father also appears fused to his daughter at their forearms. The daughter is conflicted between pulling away, as exhibited in the movement of her chest and upper torso, and being drawn towards her father as shown by her head and lower torso. Ellen is standing to the left of her mother, equal in height and thereby projecting her view that this mother is no more emotionally developed than a child or she herself is. We also note that Ellen is beginning to twist her body parallel to her mother's. This mirrors both Ellen's identification with her mother and the effects of domestic violence on the second generation.

Above the family and to the left, apparently guarding from above, yet without "a foot to stand on," is the grandmother. She looks down on her daughter and grandaughter with skewed vision, seeing them separately and visually keeping each one in her place within the family structure. The grandmother's and grandfather's diametrically opposite positions on the page, encapsulating the younger generations, serve the purpose of both locking in Ellen and

her mother and maintaining a distance between the grandparents. Ellen and her mother may, in fact, be buffers in a battle between the members of the older generation.

The immobility of Ellen's mother is graphically depicted by the omission of legs. Ellen, too, appears stuck in her own anxiety, for although she has feet they are covered by the heavily shaded floor, in which she is rooted like a plant in earth.

Above Ellen and her mother is the intense sky, seeming to fall in on them. However, ambivalence and optimism are represented by the sun that shines over the grandfather. Despite the adversarial relationship Ellen experiences between him and her mother, she apparently also sees him as an object of warmth.

An additional positive indicator in this picture is the sophisticated treatment of the figures, which are considerably detailed for the work of a six year old. Note the inclusion of eyelashes, eyebrows, torso, necks, lips, and well-defined clothing. These indicate an advanced level of cognitive development that may prove fruitful in helping Ellen negotiate her future.

Pat

Family 6

Nine-year-old Pat's drawing of her family graphically erects a barrier between the different members. To the left are Pat's older half-sisters, ages 15 and 16, both of whom have been sexually molested by Pat's father. Not only are these girls different from Pat because of the sexual abuse, but they also were fathered by another man. To the right of the partition is Pat's dad, who is sitting in profile watching television. He is not communicating with the family and has been drawn so that his two legs are fused together and his feet, too small to stand upon, do not reach the floor. The line pressure forming his lap and his legs was strong enough to tear the paper, connoting Pat's intense concern regarding the area around his genitals and his mobility. Pat may, in fact, have erected the wall to protect her sisters against his continual sexual assaults. Her father's profile position portrays Pat's view of him as a withdrawn and defiant man. Above the father, locked in with Pat, is her mother, also depicted as unable to move since she has neither legs nor feet. Pat drew herself last, as an afterthought, and although she is nine years old, in this drawing she appears as a little child, depicted in the most basic stick-like form. Interestingly, she and the encapsulated image on the television are virtually identical. Does her father view her as entertainment, and is this why she feels so small and vulnerable?

Except for the close proximity of Pat to her mother, the family members are disconnected and distant from each other. Pat described the scene as "Sandy's mad at Jill and Jill is mad at Sandy and Jill has turned her back on Sandy. My father's watching TV. My mother went shopping to the supermarket. I'm with my mother. I always go." This story reflects Pat's sense of sharing in the nurturing process with her mother. However, the two older daughters are excluded and left to make contact through fighting. This echoes the parental pattern of angry and hostile interactions and leaves us questioning these girls' abilities to develop social and interpersonal skills.

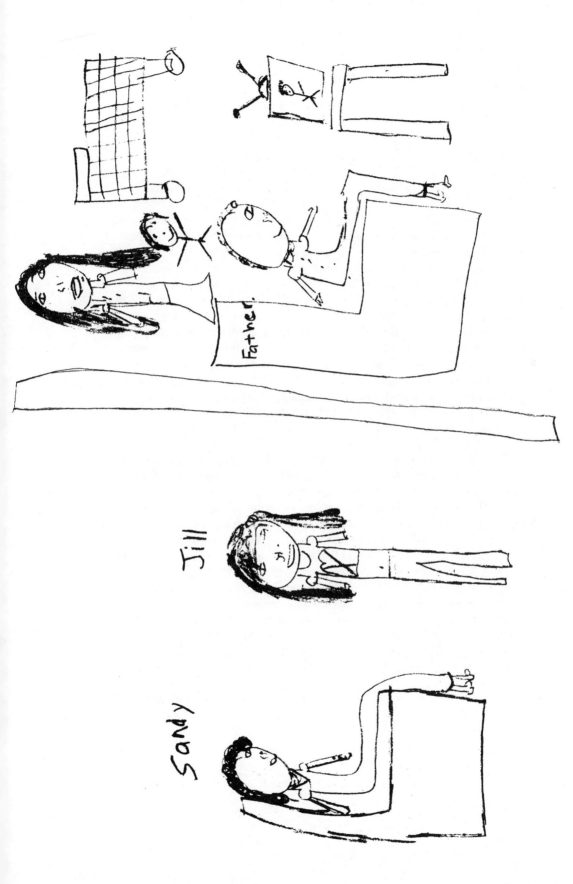

Harriet

Family 7

Harriet's Kinetic Family Drawing projects her perceptions of a number of her family's strengths. First of all, we notice that all the members are represented in heights indicative of their chronological ages. On the extreme left is the mother, Dianne, followed by two sisters, ages 13 and 11, a younger brother, age four, and on the right stands Harriet, age eight. This comparatively accurate representation tell us that Harriet experiences an appropriate designation of familial roles and responsibilities.

A second positive indication is that differences do exist even though the mother and siblings look alike. We see this in the shape of the pocketbooks worn by Dianne and her two eldest daughters. Perhaps this depiction is Harriet's way of portraying her sisters' rites of passage into adolescence. Harriet does not have a pocketbook, reflecting her younger age and earlier stage of development. The pocketbooks on the older girls are drawn with separate detailing: one is round and the other is decorated with fringe. The unique treatment of each individual, although modest, nevertheless reflects a fair amount of individuation, separation, and autonomy.

Still a third indication of relative health is the presence of most of the major body parts. In accordance with Koppitz's developmental norms for an eight-year-old girl (1968), Harriet includes all the expected body parts, with the exception of the torso, as well as many of the less common items such as fingers, hands, and two-dimensional feet. It is the authors' sense that this may reflect Harriet's perception that she and the other family members are relatively well developed. In other words, Harriet's experience gives her the impression that her mother, sisters, and brother are each okay – or, in more sophisticated language, are each progressing normally through their own developmental cycles.

Despite these positives, Harriet also unconsciously shares her sense of the familial difficulties through her drawing. As we noted above, none of the bodies has a torso. Since the body is the seat of all feelings and drives, this may suggest that the family copes with its overwhelming existence and the emotions evoked by using the defense mechanism of denial. Further evidence of the tendency to

deny painful and conflictual areas is the graphic omission of Harriet's father. No suggestion of his role as part of the family is made. Could the space between Harriet and her brother have once been filled by her father?

Continuing to look at the placement of Harriet in relation to her family, we see that she is on the extreme right of the page, further from her mother (the source of nurturance) than are the other children. She is also standing alone and apart from the rest of the family. There is more distance between her and her brother than between any other two family members. Is she standing on the side passively hoping to be noticed and taken care of? The same frail and helpless quality seen in her Human Figure Drawing (Person 9) is again portrayed here. And again, her therapist's impression of a child who watches and sees, but does not say, is confirmed.

Brian

Family 8

The grossly undersized figures in 10-year-old Brian's Kinetic Family Drawing paradoxically command immediate attention. Their smallness vehemently states his perception that his family is inadequate. Buck (1981) believes that a tiny figure can be interpreted as representing a tendency to withdraw from the outside world. Yet, using the paper as a baseline graphically demonstrates that this family needs external supports to function (Ogdon, 1981). All the figures in this drawing not only are small individually, but also collectively occupy a minimal amount of space on the paper. This tells us how overwhelming and overpowering Brian experiences his surroundings to be, and how incompetent he feels his family is in negotiating it. The placement of the family members on the bottom of the page further depicts their insecurity.

Another important facet of this drawing is the activity in which the family is involved. All the members are competing in a race and each person is out for himself or herself. Sadly, however, no one has feet, so no one can get to the finish line. Neither the parents nor the children have the capacity to move towards their individual goals. They are also unable to reach out or help each other, for they have no hands. Clearly Brian experiences this family as a group of isolated individuals who generally compete rather than cooperate.

In looking at the placement of the figures in relation to each other, note that Brian is standing between his mother and father, yet closer to his mother. In this way he is visually distancing his parents, possibly as a means of protecting his mother from his father or limiting the contact between them. This positioning may also reflect Brian's fear that he is responsible for their marital disruption.

Start

James Enid Daddy Brian Mommy Finish

James

Family 9

In James's drawing of his family, we see the members represented in a somewhat bizarre manner. The figure on the left, the father, reminds us of a helium balloon being swept away by the wind. The center armless figure, James, stands helplessly above his mother, whose heavily shaded eyes look anxiously out towards the environment. The older brother, Brian, is conspicuously absent, perhaps because James wishes to be an only child.

It is interesting to observe that the father, who lacks arms, nose, mouth, and a clearly defined body, has oversized ears. It is pertinent to remind the reader that James's father, John, who has auditory hallucinations, has been diagnosed as a paranoid schizophrenic. Clearly, James is cognizant of these problems, as they are reflected in the ears of this figure (Jolles, 1971). The tail-like appendage, which is highly unusual in a human figure drawing, suggests that James sees his father as primitive and lacking inhibitions, much like an animal.

James has positioned himself between his parents, although closer to his mother. Yet, the father's left ear, which appears extended, seems to be listening to the mother and son. It may also represent James's pitiful attempt to relate to his family. Sadly, the father has no mouth with which to speak, nor do the others have ears with which to hear him. Perhaps this is because James can no longer tolerate the verbal abuse erupting from his father and has, therefore, conveniently forgotten to include these body parts.

There is no sense of caretaking or connectedness between these family members. Rather, one receives feelings of emptiness created by the overwhelming space surrounding this family. Perhaps their isolation and their overpowering environment have helped to foster the confusion evidenced in the treatment of the eyes. Reminiscent of Kay's Human Figure Drawing (Person 1), the figures' eyes all reflect confusion and an inability to focus clearly.

Lorraine

Family 10

This Kinetic Family Drawing created by six-year-old Lorraine is particularly telling when the reader considers the comparatively advanced quality of her Human Figure Drawing (Person 5). In that picture we saw details such as a neck and necklace, eyes with pupils and brows, and a full body. However, in this portrayal of her family, Lorraine includes only heads, while also deleting some of the more specific facial features. The omission of the trunk and appendages in these family members is important since these are instruments of power with which to manipulate or be manipulated.

Hammer (1980) points out that children's perceptions of their bodies develop from the physical pains and pleasures they've experienced. Their observations of the way people use their own bodies have a significant effect on their body concepts, as do the youngsters' physical experiences with others.

Ogdon (1981) states that the body, particularly the trunk, is associated with basic drives. Maslow (1954) has identified the basic drives as being hunger, thirst, and sex. Combining Hammer's and Ogdon's interpretations, we can conclude that the limited way in which the family members are presented in Lorraine's Kinetic Family Drawing is a clear projection of her perception of the entire family's severe difficulties in satisfying their basic drives.

The father (upper left), mother (center), and children (Lorraine, right; Willy, lower left) in this family have no arms, legs, and bodies with which to make love or rape, walk or stomp, cuddle or hit. Just as we saw in Lynn's drawing (Family 1), Lorraine's drawing denies her family's ability to inflict pain, while also removing their capacity to provide nurturance.

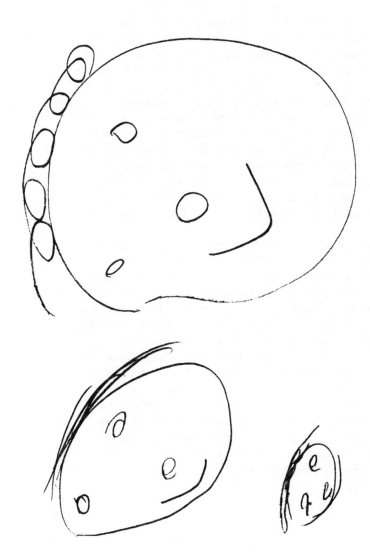

Marilyn

Family 11

In this drawing of eight-year-old Marilyn's family, we see three relatively well-developed figures, all with more detail than is generally expected to be included in a drawing by a female child of this age (Koppitz, 1968); this is indicative of Marilyn's at least average I.Q. (Harris, 1963). All rosy-cheeked and smiling, this family stands outside beneath the rays of the sun. Barely a cloud mars the sky. The scene is initially inviting, almost festive. Marilyn is even holding a balloon filled with hearts.

Marilyn describes this scene: "My father wants to tell me that it's time for lunch, and my mother is telling him to shut up because she has an ear infection, and he's screaming. He's screaming because I'm not right next to him." This short story immediately tells us that the day is not quite as sunny as a quick glance at the drawing suggests. Marilyn's father, Bob, is calling to her in order to feed her. The response of her mother, Joan, creates dissension, which Marilyn rationalizes with a feeble excuse. This narrative reveals the conflict within the family around issues of nurturance and closeness.

Although Marilyn draws her mother and father side by side, Joan is, in fact, leaning away from Bob and towards her daughter. Marilyn, in turn, leans away from her mother. If the direction of the positions were to continue into movement, we have the sense that Bob would be left standing alone in the corner. However, Marilyn perceives her mother's ambivalence towards her husband. We notice that Joan's right arm is extended towards Bob and almost touches his hand.

The position of the mother in this drawing, between Marilyn and her father, reflects the mother's use of herself as a buffer. We wonder whether this is to protect her daughter or to satisfy her own needs to be close to both her husband and daughter. Ordinarily we would interpret the position of the parents standing side by side as positive. In light of Marilyn's story, however, this is somewhat questionable.

This Kinetic Family Drawing projects Marilyn's identification with her mother. This is seen in the similar stance of both figures, in triangular dresses, and importantly, in the repetition of the hearts in the mother's dress and in Marilyn's balloon.

Of concern is the size of Marilyn's self figure in comparison to that of her parents. Obviously this eight-year-old youngster does not experience her parents as "bigger" or more grown-up than she. As she looks towards the future (right side of page), a balloon, symbolizing the love Marilyn is trying to "hold on to," seems to be slipping from her grasp.

Miriam

Family 12

This composite of five separate drawings, by five-year-old Miriam, is not a Kinetic Family Drawing. Rather, it is her response to instructions for individual projective drawings of a human figure, a person of the opposite sex, a family, a house, and a tree. These five drawings normally comprise a full battery of projective drawing tests. However, Miriam's response seriously deviates from the norm, and as such provides another important facet of analysis for us to understand.

The particular interpretation of omissions, inclusions, posture, stance, line pressure, etc., have been, and will continue to be, discussed about most of the individual drawings in this book. However, they will not be addressed here, for the most significant factor regarding these drawings is the artist's response to the drawing instructions.

Miriam began with the correct response in her first two drawings. When asked to draw a person, she drew her father (Figure 1) and next followed instructions to draw a person of the opposite sex by sketching her mother (Figure 2). However, when then asked to make a picture of a house, she continued to draw another person (Figure 3) and stated it was her sister. The next two pictures (Figures 4 and 5) were supposed to be a tree and a family, but were, instead, herself and her cousin. Miriam's manner of responding to these directives may reflect her perseveration, her opposition, and/or her need to control an anxiety-provoking situation.

It appears that Miriam became locked into a rigid pattern of thinking. This may reflect schizophrenia, learning disabilities, organicity, or a severe anxiety disorder. Based only on these projective drawings, we cannot conclusively diagnose from which of these conditions Miriam is suffering. We do know that this perseveration indicates serious pathology, and that further evaluation is imperative. Only after completion of psychological testing and neurological examination can these hypotheses be considered.

It is important, however, to be mindful of the fact that this child has witnessed a full cadre of emotional and physical marital abuse including pushing, grabbing, choking, and even rape. Unquestionably, this has severely impacted on Miriam. However, based on the current available information, we cannot determine if her difficulties are more in the sphere of organicity or intrapsychic disturbance.

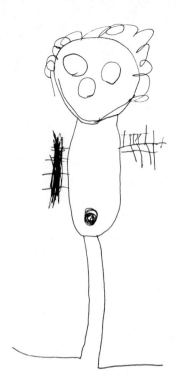

Figure 1

Figure 2

Figure 3

Figure 4

Figure 5

CHAPTER 4

THE HOUSE DRAWING

Overview

Webster defines a house as "a permanent dwelling place or living quarters; something that serves for shelter and habitation." It is within the house that the basic needs of family life, affection, and security are sought (Di Leo, 1983). Symbolically, the house serves as a self-portrait, reflecting the child's body image, maturity, adjustment, accessibility to others, contact with reality, and general emotional stability (Buck, 1981; Hammer, 1980). Experts in the field of projective drawings believe that the house also represents the child's perception of the parental home. This includes the youngster's view of his or her home life, the quality of his relationship with his family, his sense of how he is experienced by his family, and the child's attitudes concerning both his parents and siblings (Buck, 1981; Di Leo, 1983; Hammer, 1980; Ogdon, 1981).

Interestingly, the house is the child's second favorite subject to draw, after the human figure (Hammer, 1980). As such, asking a youngster to draw a picture of a house is a pleasant and nonconfrontive method by which to elicit valuable information. Di Leo (1983) cites Abbele's (1970) research of drawings by Florentine children that showed that houses appeared in 60 percent of the spontaneous drawings created by children between the ages of six and seven. However, by the age of 10 or 11 the majority of spontaneous drawings included houses only as part of the background of a scene. This change probably represents the child's

81

progression from the nest of the nuclear family to interests and relationships outside the home.

Our global impression of the house is the first step in understanding this graphic communication. This means experiencing the house and its surroundings as a whole, without regard to its individual components. Is the drawing pleasant, scary, cheerful, etc.? The next step is looking at specific factors such as size, placement, line quality and pressure, dimensionality, perspective, transparencies, and relevant, nonessential, irrelevant and bizarre details. Expected details in houses drawn by persons over six years of age include at least one door, one window, one wall, a roof, and a chimney (Buck, 1981), all of which have individual symbolic meaning. Other aspects important for consideration in the interpretation of a house are: the rooms which are included or excluded; the presence of pathways; the use of entrance details leading up to the house; and the inclusion of a groundline.

The door is representative of the child's accessibility to interpersonal contact. As an example, an open door suggests a strong need for emotional warmth; the absence of a door reflects a tendency to withdraw from the environment (Jolles, 1971). Just as eyes are our windows to the world, the windows in a house provide an eye to the environment. Windows, adequate in number and size, indicate normal personal accessibility (Hammer, 1980). The absence of windows is the child's way of saying, "I'll make it impossible for you to see in." At the same time, the youngster pays a price by not being able to see out. In understanding the symbolism communicated by the door and the windows, it is important to look at the location, number, style, size, proportion, emphasis, and details.

Walls generally connote ego strength; strong walls are equated with a sturdy ego, and thin walls with a fragile one. Overemphasized walls are attributed to the child's strong and conscious need to maintain ego control.

The chimney is both a phallus and a symbol of warmth in the youngster's close relationships. The particular treatment given to this part of the house, such as its emphasis, reinforcement, absence, size, transparency, and the number of chimneys, are all significant. The characteristics of the chimney smoke, including its presence or absence, direction, shape, and intensity, must also be considered.

Buck (1981) states that there is sound empirical evidence for the assumption that the roof symbolizes thinking and fantasy when the house is viewed as a psychological self-portrait. The relative size of the roof, in proportion to the rest of the house, tends to indicate the amount of time and energy the child devotes to fantasy. Overemphasis of the roof is most often seen in drawings by people who are afraid of losing control over their fantasy life. Conversely, the omission of a roof, or one depicted by only a single line, reflects an inability to daydream or fantasize in other ways (Hammer, 1980).

An important component of analysis of the house drawing is the Post-Drawing Interview. Jolles discusses a number of questions, which, when answered by the child, enhances and expands the data base. They include: Does that house have an upstairs? Is that your house? Would you like to own that house yourself? As you look at that house, does it seem to be close by or far away? What does that house make you think of? What does that house need most? What is the weather like?

All of the above information, when combined, offers the examiner a rich source of entry into the child's inner world. The rest of this chapter will be devoted to interpreting 15 house drawings, illustrating and highlighting the factors discussed in this overview.

Kay
House 1

   This house drawn by Kay, age five, looks like a grotesque, screaming face. As in her figure in Person 1, in which the eyes do not focus, in this drawing, too, we are unable to focus on what this house represents. Is the upper protuberance a roof or a chimney? Are the lines on the left side of the drawing windows or texture, or simply a mistake? The drawing tells us that this child does not easily allow others to get close to her. This is shown by the door, which is poorly defined as an entrance. At five years of age, most children are able to clearly draw a door and include the doorknob (Kellogg, 1970). The confusion and grotesque quality that this house represents is an accurate projection of Kay's tumultuous home environment.

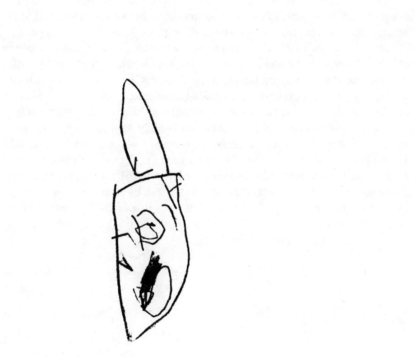

Andrew

House 2

As in Andrew's drawing of a man (Person 2), we again see this six-year-old boy's inability to interact with his environment. This empty and vacant house is devoid of windows, doors, and a path. Clearly, it offers neither security nor warmth. Neither does it allow others to come in or see in, nor Andrew to see out. The large roof represents the excessive fantasizing Andrew has created as a way of coping with a horrendous home environment. The insecure connection of the roof to the main structure of the house graphically portrays his tenuous balance between reality and fantasy. In his Human Figure Drawing Andrew paid major attention to the head. In his portrayal of a house, we see a parallel focus. However, the roof, which represents the fantasy area, is empty and vacant. Although this child is retreating from what he experiences as an unsatisfying environment, he lacks inner resources to help himself in a constructive way.

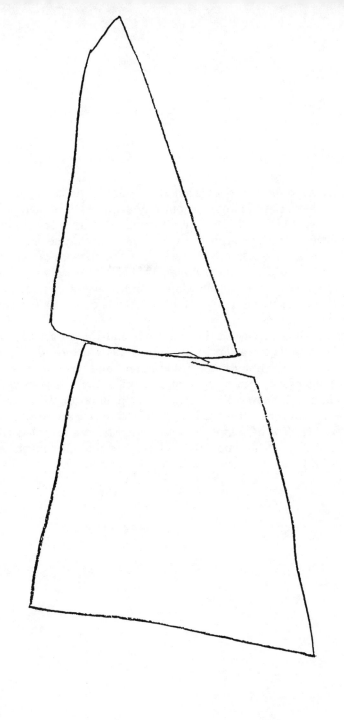

Carol

House 3

Here again, we have a sense that this building, drawn by Carol, age five, is devoid of life and without any suggestion of being a lived-in home. While we believe children who flee from their homes may deny the loss and anguish of their home environment by creating a vacant structure, it is clear that the absence of windows and door indicates a serious problem. This child has no way of looking into the environment or allowing others to see or contact her. As in Andrew's drawing, there are no windows, doors, or paths in the house.

The erratic line quality of the side walls and the progressive narrowing of the walls towards the bottom of the house reflect Carol's perception of a crumbling home environment and possibly the disintegration of her own meager coping skills. Carol is a sweet, likeable child who outwardly disguises any pain or anguish. In this house we have a sense of a top-heavy structure representing the top-heavy weight of her emotions and thoughts. We fear that this youngster may soon become overwhelmed and may no longer be able to maintain even her current level of functioning.

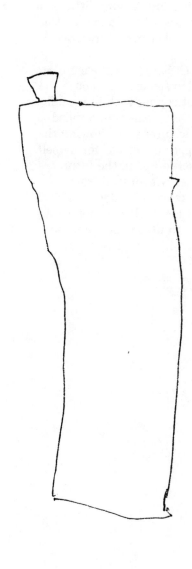

Pat

House 4

As noted in the previous House drawing, this painting is also devoid of windows, doors, and pathways. Yet here there is a sense of life. In fact, we are overcome by the intense agitation that surrounds this house. The many hands reaching out to forceably touch or stop one another may reflect nine-year-old Pat's fear of her home environment. The physical beating and sexual abuse this young girl has witnessed fill up the "atmosphere" of her life, leaving little space for anything else. Pat utilizes the bottom edge of the paper as the groundline of the house rather than creating her own drawn one, which reflects her insecurity.

This is further demonstrated by the black lines, which ensure protection against unwanted intrusion. We also see in Pat's house the intense utilization of fantasy as her way of coping with life. Unlike the vacant roof in Andrew's drawing (House 2), this roof is filled with stripes and dots of various shades and intensity, showing that she has creatively defined a substantial space of retreat for herself. However, we question how well this will serve Pat in the future. The thick black walls not only represent her withdrawal from others, but also connote her chronic depression. This depression literally "contains" the intense rage within her. This is graphically represented by the deep red that Pat used to fill the house when she produced this painting.

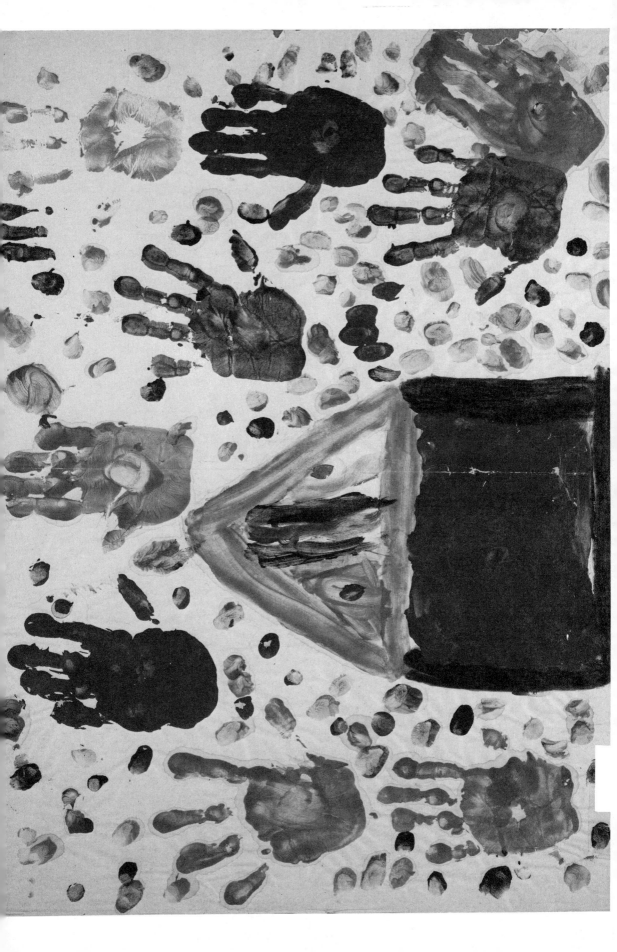

Ned

House 5

In reviewing drawings of children's houses in Kellogg's *Analyzing Children's Art* (1970), we note that the teepee-shaped house that Ned, age six, has drawn is more commonly produced by four year olds and may, in fact, represent a lag in Ned's cognitive development. In his drawing of a boy (Person 4), we pointed out that Ned has begun to constrict his environment as a way of coping with life. Notice a parallel constriction in the triangular shape of this house. We believe this also reflects his attempt to control the environmental stimulation.

The presence of a number of bare and paneless windows suggests that this is a child whose social interactions are clumsy and blunt. Yet, this youngster has drawn a well-defined door and doorknob and passively waits to "welcome" contact. However, his fusion with the doormat and pathway indicates his ambivalence. Considering Ned's life experiences with a violent father, who also is a convicted rapist, we can readily understand his anticipation of being "stepped on" as the price of contact. This boy still has some hope for the future, however, as symbolized by the smoke lightly emerging from the chimney. We are aware that this hope is tainted with trepidation, for the thin vertical lines move directly to the right (and, therefore, to the future) and become somewhat agitated in their quality.

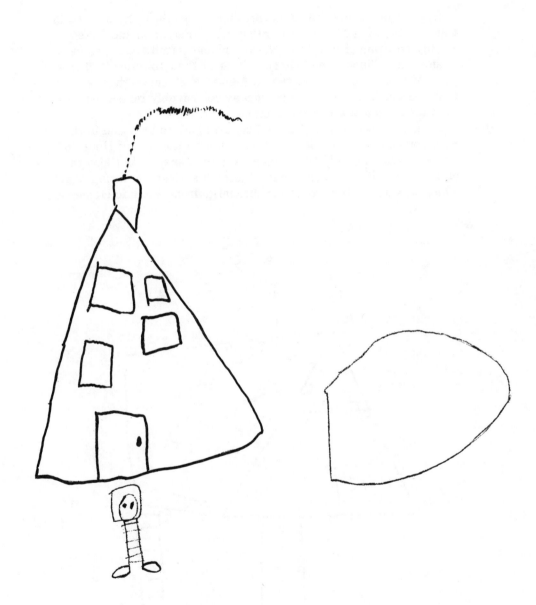

Lorraine

Houses 6 and 7

Both of Lorraine's drawings corroborate the difficulties noted in this six year old's Human Figure Drawing (Person 5) and Kinetic Family Drawing (Family 10). Neither house permits easy access. In House 6 (see illustration below), neither of the two paths lead to a door. We might guess that the path on the extreme right takes us to a rear entrance. If this is so, it may conceivably reflect her known experience with sexual abuse.

Further confirmation of sexual concerns are to be found in the numerous bananas she described as being on the roof of House 6. These include not only the rounded and oval shapes, but also the agitated scribbles as well. House 7 (see illustration on facing page), which was drawn the day of her discharge from the Safe Home, con-

firms the use of intellectual control as a way of coping with her bodily drives. This was similarly discussed in the neck treatment in Person 5. We note that the bananas on House 6 have been replaced with the words, "I love you," in House 7. This suggests control over her overwhelming feelings and a higher level of functioning. However, this functioning is not yet fully developed as she misspells "you" (a word she has spelled correctly on other occasions) as "yoy."

The door in House 7 has been doubly outlined and is larger than in House 6. This may suggest more accessibility to her personality since, as previously stated, House 7 was drawn at the end of her stay at the Safe Home, and House 6 was created at the beginning. We also note that there are more windows in the second drawing, again reflecting Lorraine's desire for increased contact. Ambivalence exists, however, since these windows are above ground level and do not allow others to easily see in. These feelings are further confirmed by the alarm system Lorraine has placed to the right of the door, which is based on the actual alarm in the Safe Home. Her meager attempt at self-protection is sadly ineffective, as the alarm is not attached to either the windows or the doors. This reflects her fear that in leaving the "Safe Home" she is in danger of severing her protection. Sadly, we are aware that House 6 appears to be precariously balanced on two stilts and that House 7 is paper-based, reflecting strong feelings of insecurity.

Jessica

House 8

This house, drawn by 11-year-old Jessica, reveals a stark and empty environment in which only a few rather unconnected flowers tentatively suggest life. The lack of windows on the ground floor, coupled with the large amount of space given to those that are drawn, mirror both this young girl's desire for contact and her tendency to withdraw from others. The absence of a path to the door further confirms her isolation. Of serious concern is the paper-chopped roof, which is seldom seen in house drawings (Jolles, 1971). This suggests that Jessica not only uses fantasy as a way of gaining satisfactions not available from others, but also utilizes it as a frantic retreat from reality. The large size of this house on the paper and the feeling of space constriction symbolize Jessica's anger and frustration.

When we compare this house with her life history, we are not surprised to find that the doorknob is very suggestive of a penis and that the chimney (also structurally shaped to be available for use as a phallic symbol) is cut off. The chimney, which not only represents warmth and intimate relationships but is also a potential phallic symbol, is a very logical target for the anger of an 11-year-old child who had been sexually abused by her stepfather for five years.

Harriet

House 9

This anthropomorphic house, resembling a face and drawn by eight-year-old Harriet, suggests regression and possible mental deficiency (Ogdon, 1981). Since it is placed on the left side of the page, well beyond the normal midpoint range for eight-year-old females (Jolles, 1971), there is the additional projection of impulsiveness, and a tendency to focus on the past. It is relevant to remind the reader at this point that Harriet's parents separated approximately one year ago and that the separation has culminated in chaos, court orders, and, finally, the family's admission into the Safe Home. It may well be that this youngster longs to return to earlier, somewhat more "normal" times.

We sense a fragile quality in this building. Somehow it is reminiscent of Harriet's Human Figure Drawing (Person 9). Perhaps it is the narrowness and the shaky sidewalls that make us feel that if this structure were a person, we might be drawn to hold and protect it. The relatively small windows, high above the main level, seem like weary eyes, neither seeing out nor giving a hint of what is within. The small door, meek and tentative in appearance, narrow at the base and giving the sense of being unhinged, doesn't allow for much entrance.

The subtle emphasis on the roof underscores this child's fragility. As we have stated earlier, the roof represents the fantasy and the intellectual area. In this picture, the carefully drawn lines across the roof project a metaphor suggestive of an attempt to put a "cap" on the area. This treatment, coupled with the paper-chopping on the top of the page, tells us that Harriet is using fantasy as a way of seeking satisfactions not obtainable from reality (Jolles, 1971). Yet, like the sidewalls of the house, the lines defining this area, particularly on the right side, are wavy and insecure. It seems that, like other children presented in this book, Harriet cannot even escape successfully into fantasy.

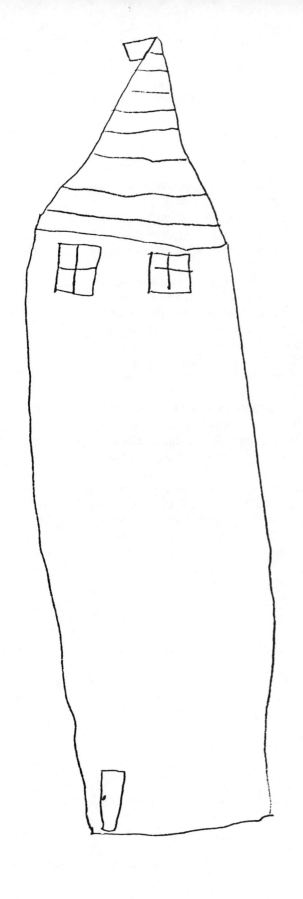

Brian

House 10

This house drawn by 10-year-old Brian reflects his well-developed ego. This is demonstrated by the strong sidewalls and the consistently firm and solid quality of the lines used (Jolles, 1971). However, the long strokes also suggest the probability of controlled actions that at times may lead to his inhibited behavior (Ogdon, 1981).

Looking further at the details of the house we notice the elaborately decorated chimney. The repetitive pattern in the numerous bricks alerts us to the level of Brian's anxiety concerning his need to control his virility (Ogdon, 1981). This is further confirmed by the enlarged top on the chimney, which serves to contain and hold down these feelings. This reminds us of the baldheaded man in Brian's Human Figure Drawing in which these issues were also raised.

Brian's differential treatment of the windows on the first floor from those on the second and third floors illustrates his vulnerability in close interpersonal situations. Perhaps this is due to the erratic and dangerous behavior his father exhibited before the family's admission to the Safe Home. Brian defends against his sense of vulnerability by placing elaborate curtains on ground-floor windows. However, those on the upper levels, which are less accessible, are barren and indicate his readiness to make contact from a distance (Jolles, 1971). His need for distance is further confirmed by the absence of a path leading to the door.

James

House 11

This sharply angled house drawn by James reveals his perceived lack of familial balance. Koppitz (1968) states that the slanting of a figure by more than 15 degrees in the Human Figure Drawing occurs most frequently in drawings of insecure, unstable children who lack emotional balance. It is the authors' belief that this same principle can be applied to interpreting house drawings. Since the drawing of a house has been acknowledged as tapping the artist's attitudes about family life (Hammer, 1980), the angle of the house should therefore project the experienced degree of family stability. James's family is on the edge of collapse, much like this house.

The second outstanding feature in this house is the number of holes permeating the base. We also note there are neither windows nor doors on this main living level. These factors reflect a profound sense of emptiness and isolation. More importantly, the holes suggest that the solidity of James's family life has been extracted piece by piece.

A third important point is the enlarged roof, which weighs heavily on the base. This may be seen as James's creative solution of using fantasy to compensate for his losses. We also see windows in the attic leading us to believe that one can gain access to James by joining with him in his fantasies. The strong lines defining the sidewalls of the house represent ego strength (Ogdon, 1981) and are the first suggestion that James does possess some limited resources with which to cope.

Simon

House 12

This one-dimensional house drawn by 10-year-old Simon reminds us of a stage set. The house appears as a veneer of reality – a façade to the outside world – echoing the mask behind which his family hid. In addition, despite the presence of seven windows, which would normally suggest personal accessibility (Hammer, 1980), one has a sense that there is no one in this house with whom to have contact.

The barred windows on the upper level connote imprisonment. Since these windows are almost in the roof area, it may be that Simon's fantasies are barred from his consciousness. The hasty line quality evidenced in the treatment of the window panes suggests impulsivity. Thoughts and fantasies are the way a healthy person mediates action. If, in fact, Simon is cut off from this part of himself, then his options for problem solving are limited. The excessive space given to the bare windows in this house point to Simon's direct, blunt behavior (Ogdon, 1981) and the coarseness of his social interactions. These factors combined may explain Simon's acting-out behavior as observed in the Safe Home.

This very large house, which fills the page, projects Simon's use of overcompensation as a way of coping with his negative feelings about himself. This defense mechanism is reminiscent of the superhero drawn by Simon (Person 12), although the size of the person drawing was small. In both situations, exaggerations are utilized to counterbalance feelings of inadequacy.

Simon's difficulty with gender identification reappears in his house drawing. As stated throughout this text, the chimney is a well-accepted symbol of masculinity. Its omission clearly represents Simon's problems in dealing with the male sex symbol (Jolles, 1971) and may also indicate his castration fears (Landisberg, 1969). This issue appeared in Simon's Human Figure Drawing and resurfaces here attesting to its intensity.

One final point about the chimney is the additional interpretation that this structure is a barometer that reflects the degree of family warmth (Jolles, 1971). Its absence, therefore, helps to confirm the lack of positive nurturance experienced by Simon in his family.

Blanche

House 13

This paper-based and paper-chopped house drawn by eight-year-old Blanche alerts us to several noteworthy factors. As stated earlier in this text, the paper upon which the artwork is drawn represents the environment. As such, when an artist uses the paper as a means of providing a baseline for the drawing, he or she is projecting excessive dependence. Even though it is expected that an elementary-school-age child be dependent, only two of the preceding 11 houses we have presented do rest on the bottom of the page as a way of stabilizing the structure. It is, therefore, significant that this child has chosen to ground her house in this manner.

In light of several major family traumas, Blanche's inordinate dependence can be understood. Her family history includes an early separation from her natural father, followed by several years of instability, and culminates in being witness to an abusive marital relationship between her mother and stepfather. During this violent period, which lasted for approximately three years, she, too, was harassed and attacked by her stepfather. To quote Blanche, "Because my stepfather got mad, he broke two windows, and came up in my room. He said he was going to rape me. Mom said, 'Don't touch her,' but hid in her own room. Joseph [her stepfather] took a lamp and swung it at my head."

This anecdote exemplifies countless episodes of violence, trauma, and crisis. It also helps to explain the placement and paper-chopping of Blanche's house on the right side of the page. Jolles's explanation (1971) of these phenomena is that they project a desire to escape into the future by getting away from the past, and represent a tendency to exercise strong emotional control.

This emotional restraint is also reflected in Blanche's treatment of the grass, which serves to fence in the house. The sharp, pointed blades inhibit entry and press against the phallic-shaped door. This scene is poignantly reminiscent of the following statement about her stepfather made by Blanche during the discussion after completion of the projective drawings: "A long, long time ago, he called me into the kitchen while I was getting dressed and he picked me up and he pulled down his pants. He couldn't get in so he left. Mommy was at work. Last summer, and many times before that, he said, 'Touch it.'"

Dennis

House 14

This house, drawn by 11-year-old Dennis, is painful to the eye of the experienced interpreter. Seen from below, it projects feelings of rejection and unhappiness in the home. Sadly, happiness in Dennis's family is considered unattainable by him (Buck, 1981; Hammer, 1980; Jolles, 1971). Details of this boy's family history substantiate reasons in support of his gloomy perceptions.

His mother, June, reported an 11-year history of abuse when admitted to the Safe Home. The domestic violence began during her pregnancy with Dennis. Her husband, Dennis Sr., a police sergeant, was and is an extremely abusive, active alcoholic. He has threatened her with guns and carried a knife, which he brandished in her face. He has also pushed, punched, and kicked her. The boy has witnessed much of this abuse and has himself been allegedly mistreated by both parents. Dennis Sr. claims that June has smacked the child in the face and hit him with a stick; June maintains that her husband has tried to strangle her son many times and has also taken him to local bars.

The drawing of this house very much captures the misery of Dennis's home. One of the ways in which he tries to cope with this situation is by his conscious attempt to maintain self-control. This is reflected in the double reinforcement of the sidewalls of the house's main structure (Jolles, 1971).

This house, placed high on the page, suggests Dennis's fear of the environment, and his desire to avoid conflict. The groundline, sloping downward and away from the house on both sides, reflects his feelings of isolation and exposure (Jolles, 1971). The drawing of this building conjures images of a haunted house on a hill, with clouds looming perilously from above. The bare windows, omitted chimney, heavy lines of the house and hill, and the agitated lines defining the clouds and those within the hill, all combine to create a replica of the nightmare that Dennis has lived.

Marilyn
House 15

Marilyn, age eight, has drawn a transparent house. This is noteworthy since it is the only house of this type seen in our review of 40 house drawings by the children living in the Safe Home. Di Leo (1983), in *Interpreting Children's Drawings*, correlates Piaget's developmental stages of the progression of thought to its parallel representation in a drawing. He states that in the Preoperation Stage, ages four to seven, transparencies may be drawn. At this point in a child's life, the youngster views the world egocentrically and visually reflects this by literally externalizing his or her internal model onto the paper. The transparency or X-ray technique, in which the interior of the house is seen through the walls, merely mirrors the child's egocentricity, and his or her sense that what he or she feels and sees is experienced by others in exactly the same way at the same moment.

Beginning at age seven, according to Piaget, the child enters the stage of Concrete Operations. The youngster is now able to think logically, and is not dominated by immediate perceptions. Generally, egocentric thought is no longer present at this time, and drawings will be more realistic.

It is significant that Marilyn, at age eight, has drawn a house in which the interior is exposed. Clinical observations, as well as her Human Figure (Person 15) and Kinetic Family Drawing (Family 11), all substantiate that Marilyn is of at least average intelligence. Therefore, although this transparency does not reflect an intellectual developmental lag, there is clearly a developmental arrest. We believe that this arrest is due to an emotional problem and is more than likely attributable to the domestic violence Marilyn witnessed in her home.

In assessing the nature of Marilyn's emotional problem as reflected through the drawing of the transparent house, we turn to Ogdon (1981), who offers a number of possible interpretations. They include psychosis, organicity, mental deficiency, and a compulsive need to structure situations. As noted above, we have ruled out mental deficiency. In selecting the most appropriate of the remaining hypotheses, we wish to remind the reader of our statements in the overview to children's drawings in Chapter 1. Specifically, one must consider many factors, including a review of the total battery

of projective drawings, the family history, and any other available data, before reaching a conclusive diagnosis.

Ogdon's (1981) hypothesis that a transparency in the walls represents a compulsive need to structure situations seems to be the most appropriate for Marilyn. We arrive at this conclusion based on our observation of two factors. There is an excessive use of detail, as well as repetition of patterns, in all of Marilyn's projective drawings. These characteristics, particularly when they appear together, reflect a high level of anxiety and an attempt to contain it. We have also observed Marilyn's exaggerated need to structure play therapy sessions at the Safe Home. Typically, Marilyn would begin her hour by stating which game she would start with, which art material she would use next, how long cleanup would take, and which doll she would choose if there were time left.

Jolles (1971) contends that pathological significance may be gauged by the number of transparencies, their magnitude, and their location. He further states that a transparency in the wall of a house is a strong indicator of emotional disturbance. Expanding on this concept, it is the authors' belief that the location of the transparencies within the house reflects a problem related to either the actual room or its symbolic significance. The living room and one bedroom are included in the X-ray of Marilyn's house.

The living room is the place in a home where family members typically interact. The erasures and the excessive attention to design on the couch in Marilyn's living room depict anxiety and the concomitant need to contain it. The picture of the clown hanging on the wall suggests a sense of ridicule and mockery. The fact that Marilyn not only draws the clown, but also labels and frames it, speaks to the intensity of these feelings and her need to literally box them in.

One final point about this drawing is the choice of a bedroom as the other room exposed for viewing. The heavily shaded bed (possibly reflecting anxiety about sleep), bound by arrow-like headboard and footboard, creates an uninviting and ominous atmosphere. This room, which can ordinarily provide a place for rest, comfort, and warmth, projects none of these feelings. Since this bedroom is placed in the attic, the area representing fantasy in a house drawing, we regretfully conclude that even in Marilyn's imagination there is no retreat from her pointed distress.

CHAPTER 5

THE TREE DRAWING

Overview

References to trees dot the pages of traditional literature, mythology, poetry, and children's stories. The tree, in its most basic symbolic meaning, has represented life and growth from earliest times. Recognizing its relevance, Koch (1952) developed the drawing of a tree into a projective instrument in order to obtain information about the personality of the artist.

Ogdon (1981) states that after the age of seven trees appear less affected by intelligence and emotional development than other projective drawings. Although in analyzing the drawing of a person created by a nine year old we would take developmental norms for that particular age group into account, this would not be the case for the interpretation of a tree drawn by this same child. In the latter, the guidelines for analysis remain constant.

As is true in drawings of persons and houses, elements in the personality are also projected in the way the child draws a tree and its parts. Hammer (1980) states that when a tree is drawn, deeper levels of the personality are reached and expressed than in the person drawings. The tree, a natural and vegetative form, taps basic and longstanding feelings. Interestingly, drawings of trees are less likely to change when redrawn after periods of short-term psychotherapy than those of houses and persons. This has been demonstrated by children whose situations improved over time but whose tree renderings showed only minor changes in the

113

deeper layers of the underlying personality structure. More intensive treatment was necessary before such central personality alteration was projected onto the tree drawing.

In drawing a tree, the child unconsciously selects from the many trees he or she has seen the one that most reflects his or her inner feelings about him- or herself. By allowing ourselves to experience the total gestalt of the tree, without focusing on the details, we can understand the inner picture of the youngster's life. For example, does the tree seem full in rich summer bloom or barren as in winter? Is it sturdy or about to topple? Does it appear to be desolate?

As in Human Figure and House drawings, we look at not only the totality of the drawing, but also the essential details. In the drawing of a tree, we expect the inclusion of a trunk and at least one branch (Buck, 1981). Naturally, there is infinite variation in the way these two essential details are drawn. It is, in fact, the variation that provides insight to the artist's discrete personality.

The trunk represents feelings of basic power and inner strength (Bolander, 1977; Buck, 1981), much the same as the torso does in the Human Figure Drawing. For example, reinforced peripheral lines in the trunk reflect the child's perceived need to maintain personal intactness (Hammer, 1980). Scars or holes placed at a particular point in the trunk mirror the age at which trauma was experienced, with the base of the tree viewed as the beginning of the youngster's life and the top of its trunk as his or her current age.

The branch structure has been associated with the ability to derive satisfaction from the environment, much like the hands in a Human Figure Drawing (Hammer, 1980). Falling branches may suggest the possible loss of ability to cope with environmental pressures (Buck, 1981). Well-organized and well-formed branches suggest normal flexibility and satisfactory adjustment (Ogdon, 1981).

The roots project the instinctual aspects of the personality (Buck, 1973), and are indices of personal stability (Ogdon, 1981). Roots are literally the foothold of the tree. Those that taper easily into the ground reflect good contact with reality and healthy development. Conversely, roots seen through the groundline mirror a serious flaw in reality-testing and may indicate psychosis or organicity (Jolles, 1971).

The type of tree, the leaves, and the manner in which the bark and crown are drawn are also significant factors to consider in in-

114

terpretation. For example, apple trees represent dependency; a cloud-like crown suggests active fantasy and a low energy level (Ogdon, 1981).

Additional information is gathered through the post-drawing interrogation. As stated earlier in this text, this period of questioning provides the artist with an opportunity to define, describe, change, and embellish his or her work. Of the many potential questions that have been posed in this phase, the authors have found the following to be among the most useful: What kind of a tree is this? What is its best part? Its worst part? What does this tree need the most? Is it healthy? Is it alive or dead? Does it have seeds? What is the weather like? Where is the tree located?

As with the house, person, and family drawings, the size, placement, line quality, inclusion of extraneous detail, use of a ground-line, etc., are additional relevant factors, all of which provide a foundation on which the assessment of the tree drawing should be made.

Simon

Tree 1

The initial message we receive in looking at the tree drawn by Simon, age eight, is a statement, "Notice me; I'm here." Placed directly in the middle of the page, the tree also portrays this youngster's feelings of insecurity and rigidity, and his tendency to maintain psychological equilibrium by careful control. While the trunk is drawn with a firm line, it is rather narrow for a tree so full of leaves. Di Leo (1983) states that the trunk, which is typically emphasized up to age seven, represents the preponderance of emotional life in a child. This long and narrow trunk leans slightly to the left and doesn't adequately balance the hidden branch system. It alerts us to Simon's constricted feelings and weak sense of his own power. It also reflects the fragility he experiences in balancing his needs with his ability to receive satisfaction from others. Simon has witnessed his mother being repeatedly tied up, raped, and beaten by his stepfather. Simon himself has been bound and beaten with a cord so severely that he has extensive lacerations over his back and legs. When his mother attempted to protect him, it would precipitate another abusive incident.

We are also struck by the fruits surrounding the upper portion of the tree. Fruits are commonly drawn by children, particularly those at age seven. However, they are generally drawn unattached until the child reaches age 14 (Di Leo, 1983). The fruits on Simon's tree are not only attached but seem to be standing upright, almost like a child waving his arms, pleading to be seen. Jolles (1971) has stated that apple trees are frequently drawn by dependent children and that falling apples reflect a child's feelings of rejection. The fruits on this tree certainly are not falling, and we sense that they mirror Simon's desperate cry not to be rejected, not to be thrown off.

Lorraine

Tree 2

This drawing, like others of Lorraine in this book, is additional confirmation of the severe problems this six-year-old girl experiences. We are struck immediately by the agitation and anxiety portrayed. Heavy shading under the tree, coupled with the elaborate base, tells us there are very strong feelings of insecurity and a lack of "rootedness" or "groundedness." The tree leaning towards the left, but not falling, and resting on a rocker base, reminds us of a Bop Bag, the blow-up toy one hits to knock down, but which always rights itself. At the same time, Lorraine does not seem to be in imminent danger of collapsing.

Yet the branch structure of the tree, that part which reflects her intellectual capacity and ability to secure satisfactions from others (Hammer, 1980), is poorly defined. There is no clear sense of organization and the curled lines run downward, almost reflecting a withdrawal into herself. Of significance are the fruits that top this tree. Unlike those created by most youngsters, these fruits are coconuts, from which it is very difficult to get milk or juice.

The "1,000,000" on the upper left of the page, the age Lorraine gave to the tree, serves to signify the heavy weight of her emotional life. In addition, when turned upside down Lorraine's tree clearly resembles an erect penis complete with testicles, pubic hair, and semen. Such suggestions of the sexual molestation, which were discussed in Person 5, have repeatedly shown up in Lorraine's play therapy at the Safe Home.

1,000,000

Jessica

Tree 3

As in Jessica's Human Figure Drawing (Person 8), this tree impresses us initially as having a quality of charm. Our eye is attracted to the delightful animal protectively nestled within the tree. Yet, unlike the animals shown peeking out from a tree hole that are commonly drawn by children (Ogdon, 1981), this squirrel suggests the total protection of the fetus in utero. Generally, we would interpret this to mean Jessica desires the warmth and caring associated with this fetal state. However, we must pay attention to the strong lines that separate the trunk into two roots, and the subroot structure, which looks very much like a penetrating organ. The trunk clearly resembles two legs forcibly spread apart as in rape.

Integrating 11-year-old Jessica's history of being raped by her stepfather for the past five years and the points just mentioned, we see a graphic portrayal of this experience. The lines above the subroot, or penis, are doubly reinforced and strong as if warding off further penetration. The small squirrel may very well be telling us of Jessica's concern about pregnancy and her need to be mothered and protected from continued sexual abuse. The placement of the "hole" in the trunk is also noteworthy because it occurs at the approximate midpoint of the tree. This hole, which is a scar in the tree's main support, indicates a physical or psychic experience regarded as traumatic. If we assume that the height of the tree represents Jessica's age (Hammer, 1980), the hole reflects a serious injury at approximately age five and a half; the effect of the rapes over the past five years is poignantly reconfirmed.

The faint lines delineating and filling the trunk of the tree indicate an additional area of concern, for they connote this child's lack of emotional strength, and her strong feelings of inadequacy and anxiety (Jolles, 1971). The shading in the trunk, which moves up into the areas of the branches and is covered over with apples, provides us with a powerful message. Jessica's inability to receive satisfaction from the environment is represented by the hidden branch system. Her strong need for nurturing is symbolized by the abundant apples, which reflect her maternal dependency.

Another noteworthy detail is the swing, suggestive of fun and charm, yet tenuously hanging from the end of a faintly drawn branch. The swing, which is on the right side of the page and thus projects Jessica's view of the future, is both rigid and unstable.

120

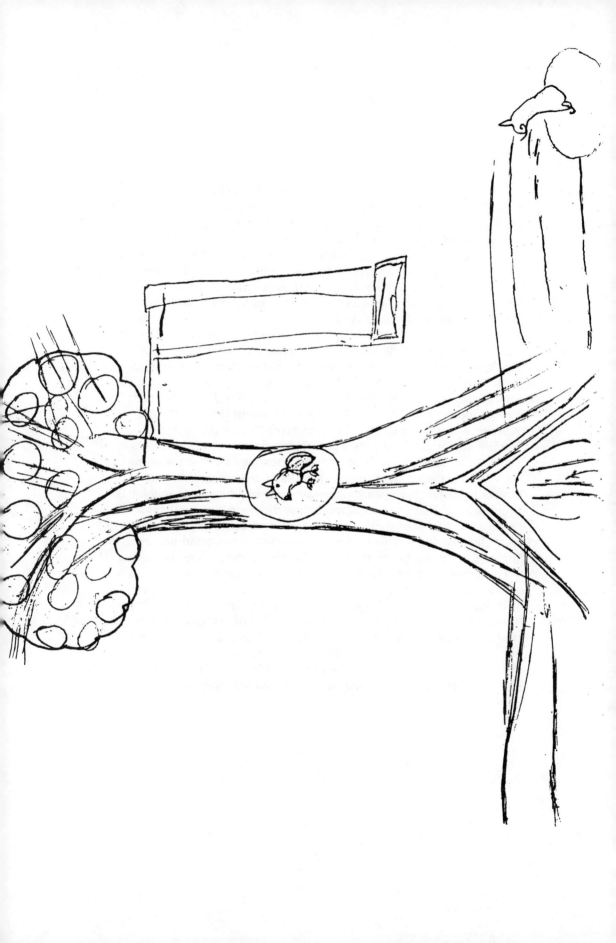

Harriet

Tree 4

This tree, drawn by eight-year-old Harriet, reminds us of her house (House 9). Placed on the left side of the page, it tells us she is focusing on the past. Another similarity between these two pictures is the treatment given to the roof of the house and the crown of the tree. In both drawings these areas contain the most detail. In addition, as noted earlier, Harriet attempts to put a cap on her fantasy by the stylized roof on her house, and by its placement. Likewise, in her Tree drawing she flattens the crown, projecting a denial or rejection of fantasy (Ogdon, 1981).

The tree is paper-based on the bottom of the page and indicates Harriet's feelings of insecurity and inadequacy (Hammer, 1980). This tree, in clinging to the edge of the paper, clues us in to Harriet's need to compensate for these emotions by passively using the environment to ground her. Just as indicated our discussion of Harriet's personality in her Human Figure Drawing (Person 9), this is another reflection of the way she counterbalances the lack of familial nurturance and gets what she needs.

One final point about Harriet's tree drawing is the sense of encapsulation created by drawing the tree in one continuous, unbroken line; the only opening is paper-based. We sense that a lot is being held in; there are no branches reaching out, no opportunity for this child to actively derive satisfaction from interpersonal contact. Unfortunately, this is typical for children reared in homes with domestic violence. Often the family is very isolated. The youngsters are encouraged to remain close to the home and are taught to be suspicious of outsiders.

Happily, the lines defining the trunk of the tree are the strongest in the drawing and mirror the basic strength of Harriet's personality. In addition, the apples are still attached to the crown projecting her felt attachment to her family. Moreover, they tend to fade "out of the picture" as we move from left (past) to right (future) representing Harriet's growing maturity towards independence.

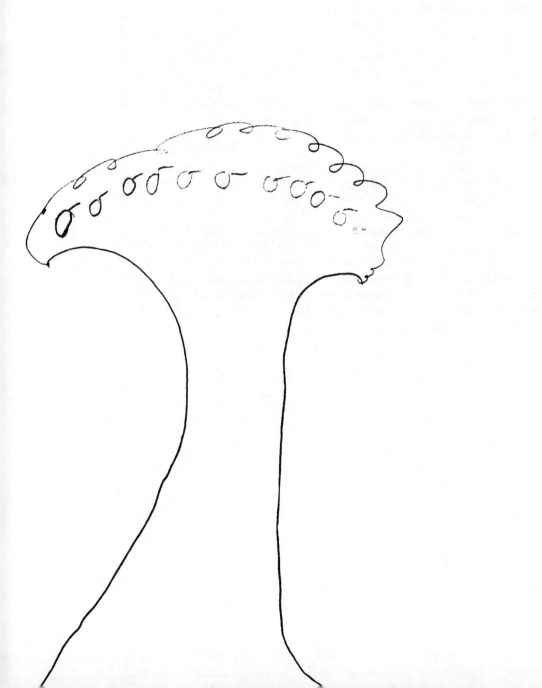

Brian

Tree 5

This tree drawn by 10-year-old Brian projects feelings of alienation, emptiness, and deprivation. Although there is a suggestion of leaves, a pervasive sense of lifelessness prevails. Also, since roots provide groundedness and a means of receiving nurturance and sustenance, their omission reflects both Brian's instability and his lack of connection to the environment.

The tree's thin trunk suggests this boy's tenuous sense of his own inner strength and power (Hammer, 1980). The empty knothole, slightly above the center of the trunk, signifies damage to the tree (Ogden, 1981). It may be that Brian was somehow traumatized at about age six. What the specific occurrences were are unknown, although his father's verbal abuse was progressively intensifying at that time. It is clear, by the size of the hole, that the events that occurred around Brian's seventh year have had resounding effects upon his life.

Since the scar extends to the circumference of the trunk, it thereby weakens it. Keeping in mind that the trunk represents the ego, we suspect that from approximately age six to seven Brian had some serious difficulties negotiating his inner and outer worlds. However, it is also important to observe that the integrity of the lines defining the trunk were not affected and, although they tend to be somewhat rigid, they are also strong and consistent. In addition, the width of the trunk does not falter as a result of the trauma. We can therefore conclude that although Brian has been deeply and negatively affected by the occurrences in his life, his basic ego strengths remain intact.

Blanche

Tree 6

We are initially struck by the large size of this tree, the agitated quality of the continuous circular line within the trunk hole, and the pointed, weapon-like blades of grass. Eight-year-old Blanche repeats several projections in her third drawing.

The sexual abuse discussed in House 13 resurfaces in the line treatment within the knot. Hammer (1980) states that holes placed by children in the tree trunk, which have animals peeping from them, may depict yearning for a withdrawn, warm, protected, uterine existence. It is the authors' belief that the omission of the animal in this knot and the substitution of a spiral line drawn towards its own center reflect Blanche's depression regarding her inability to escape into a safe, uterine environment. They further imply agitation and anxiety regarding sexual penetration.

The largeness of the tree implies a desire to defy authority figures (Ogdon, 1981). This may be a healthy sign for Blanche, particularly if this defiance relates to her stepfather. Another expression of self-protection is the repeated presence of pointed blades of grass. The reader may recall our discussion about them in House 13. Blanche again surrounds her projected image with a defensive barrier. This tells us she has good survival instincts, a necessary fortification prior to her entry into the Safe Home. The danger, however, lies in the possibility that Blanche may overgeneralize her negative parental experiences to future relationships. Therapeutic intervention is essential at this time in order to prevent future isolation that may result from her perceived need for self-protection.

Dennis

Tree 7

This "old, old, old tree" drawn and described by 11-year-old Dennis is "about to die, but maybe it won't. There was another tree," he states, "but it died. This tree is 50. Trees can't get past 50. A tree in my back yard is 100 years old. The whole thing is about to die."

From this brief narrative we hear Dennis's morbidity and his sense of impending doom. This is particularly frightening since Dennis verbalized suicidal ideations during his stay at the Safe Home. Dennis told his therapist that he would like to die and wondered how it would feel to jump from a window 10 flights up. We also note that in his story Dennis refers to three trees—one which is dead, and one which is about to die. The fate of the tree in the drawing, however, is in question.

In this story, Dennis is alluding to his family. We can speculate that the dead tree represents his mother who is self-absorbed, immobilized in bed with a variety of psychosomatic symptoms, and, therefore, unavailable to her son. The tree in Dennis's backyard, about to die at age 100, may be his father, who is the only family member remaining in the home. The fact that it is "about to die" may reflect Dennis's anger at his father and a wish that his father die. Finally, the tree depicted in this drawing symbolizes Dennis, who toys with the idea of killing himself and is uncertain as to whether he will live or die. Analysis of the actual drawing further confirms the depth of his despair.

The branches of this tree give the appearance of being either inadequately developed or cut back. Branches are symbolic of personality organization and the ability to literally reach out into the environment for satisfaction (Buck, 1981; Hammer, 1980; Jolles, 1971). The upper branches, contained in the crown of this tree, are one-dimensional and are inadequately attached to the two-dimensional trunk. This suggests that although Dennis's early psychological development was sufficient, serious trauma later in his childhood interfered with his emotional growth. This has resulted in insufficient ego strength and an inability to incorporate into his psychological fabric any nurturing qualities from his parents (Jolles, 1971). One final item to note about the upper branch structure is the scribbled lines covering it, which indicates confusion, excitement, impulsivity, and emotional instability (Koch, 1952).

The lower branches flanking the trunk present an important contrast to those above. They are two-dimensional, are more developed, and are satisfactorily connected to the trunk. Both lower branches and the trunk contain holes that represent psychological injury. However, we note that the integrity of the lines forming the trunk remains undisturbed, confirming the hypothesis that Dennis's early development was adequate.

Repeating the theme seen in Dennis's Human Figure Drawing (Person 14) is the appearance of three clouds. Once again, two of the clouds are touching, while the other, placed on the right side of the page, appears headed towards the future alone (Buck 1981).

The two figures, hanging from bars attached to a swing-like object which is tenuously connected to the right branch of the tree, may be another projection of how Dennis experiences his family. We see two pathetic people, disconnected from each other, yet hanging on. Above and between them is a hole, perhaps filling the space originally occupied by the father. This issue is so powerful a force in Dennis's psyche that it is repeated in this tree drawing.

Marilyn

Tree 8

Marilyn's compulsive personality style is revealed once more in this drawing of a tree, as it was in Person 15, Family 11, and House 15. Shapiro (1965), in *Neurotic Styles*, describes the Anxiety Disorder categorized as Obsessive-Compulsive (American Psychiatric Association, 1980). This disorder is characterized by high levels of anxiety and such an extensive preoccupation with technical details that the full flavor of experiences is missed. Shapiro delineates the three basic components of this diagnostic category as rigidity, the expression and experience of autonomy, and the loss of reality.

He explains rigidity as a literally and figuratively stiff body posture. In viewing this tree as a representation of Marilyn, we see a trunk created with such rigidity that it appears to have been drawn with a ruler. The flowers flanking the tree on both sides are, likewise, stiff and stilted.

In his discussion about the aspects of autonomy and its behavioral expression, Shapiro states that the kinds of activities in which this personality type engages are intense, concentrated, and excessive. Intensity and concentration are graphically expressed by Marilyn in the especially deep shading of the tree trunk, as well as the confused jumble of scribbled lines in the tree crown. The inordinate amount of extraneous details surrounding the tree and the repetition of the birds and balloons represent her tendency to be excessive.

The repetitive use of detail noted in all of Marilyn's drawings is her way of avoiding the anxiety related to the openness of the unknown. Like Dennis in his Human Figure Drawing (Person 14), Marilyn attempts to gain control over an overwhelming environment by compulsively filling in the spaces. However, a glaring emptiness shouts from the open hole of the tree, much like a mouth screaming.

The third characteristic of the obsessive-compulsive style discussed by Shapiro is the loss of reality. In fact, Shapiro seems to be

describing a distortion of reality and gives the example of a person who worries about things that are not merely unlikely, but truly absurd, and which, in the extreme, border on the delusional. We see a graphic depiction of this characteristic in the flowers Marilyn compulsively drew on the left side of the page, and which she described as being "just designs, not real flowers," almost, in fact, as if they are delusions. We also notice that three balloons, possibly portraying her mother, father, and self, are unattached and, symbolically, becoming increasingly ungrounded and lost as they float away.

We can conclude from the anxiety depicted in this drawing of a tree, as well as in her other projective drawings, that Marilyn defends against an overwhelming and painful reality. Unfortunately, she has already incorporated clearly dysfunctional traits into her core personality structure. The result is that she loses the full flavor of her life because the totality is more than she can handle.

CHAPTER 6

WHAT WE LEARNED

Over and over again, throughout the 50 drawings discussed, we have seen serious emotional disturbances expressed through these drawings of human figures, families, houses, and trees. The repeated projections of the 18 elementary-school-age children whose drawings have been presented mirror feelings of helplessness, powerlessness, fragmentation, depression, anger, and anxiety. The youngsters are frightened, sometimes terrified, often confused, and insecure. Their sense of self is poorly defined and their self-esteem is pitifully low. Their feelings are often denied and reality is distorted. Within the drawings are strong indications of social isolation, a lack of trust, and a general fearfulness of interpersonal contact. Of the 18 children presented, 21% reveal sexual abuse. Others show a serious preoccupation and overconcern with sexual issues.

The drawings of their families have graphically depicted the children's perceptions of family life as disconnected, lacking in nurturance, and not meeting the children's dependency needs. The families are unable to effectively control or change their environments, and are experienced by the children as inconsistent, unreliable, and unstable. Significantly, the primary mode of social interactions in these families involves anger and aggression.

Although anger can be a healthy and integral part of family life, violence is an exaggerated and pathological expression of that anger (Bowlby, 1983). According to Hershey (1982), 55 to 60 percent of all marital partners have been violent towards one another, in some form, during their married life.

Violence is thought of as a motor expression of powerlessness. We have observed that the women who have lived in the Safe Home are involved with men who generally feel powerless. In addition, neither the women nor the men have developed the skills to communicate effectively. The men, in particular, have learned to act and react impulsively, and often with physical abuse.

The effects of spouse abuse on the offspring have become of concern to the professional community only in the last 10 years. Research in this area, however, still remains in its infancy. One pair of researchers, Porter and O'Leary (1980), has found a statistically significant correlation between spouse abuse of the parents, and Conduct Disorders for preteenage boys. A Conduct Disorder is

> a repetitive and persistent pattern of conduct in which either the basic rights of others or major age-appropriate societal norms or rules are violated. The conduct is more serious than the ordinary mischief and pranks of children and adolescents. (American Psychiatric Association, 1980, p. 45)

Behaviorally, this type of disorder is often manifested in truancy, delinquency, stealing, excessive lying, aggressive behavior, and, in some cases, an inability to form meaningful friendships or to develop trust in others. A number of these components have repeatedly manifested themselves in the Safe Home children's artwork, their clinical case histories, and their therapy sessions.

In many cases, the description of Conduct Disorder closely correlates with the behavior of the boys, as well as with that of their fathers. The boys may be internalizing the anger of their fathers and appear, through their own behavior, to be identifying with the aggressor. This has been further confirmed in drawings presented earlier (i.e., Person 4, Family 4). It is important to realize that Conduct Disorders in male children have the propensity to become Antisocial Personality Disorders in adult men if effective interventions are not made.

The artwork presented (e.g., Person 1, House 4), as well as play therapy sessions at the Safe Home, have revealed that the girls tend to internalize both their own anger and that of the household. This leads to feelings of helplessness and depression (e.g., Person 3, 5, and 7). Moore (1975) noted that female children who had witnessed domestic violence have psychosomatic concerns and symptoms that include eczema, headaches, stomachaches, and a general "failure to thrive." Brown, Pelkowitz, and Kaplan (1983) have confirmed this finding.

Characteristically, mothers who have been physically abused live difficult lives, in which they are continually victimized. As a result, they often have no energy to give affection or emotional support to their children. This lack of nurturance has obvious long-term negative effects on the child, who becomes frustrated, and this often leads to aggressive behavior.

Through the use of projective drawings, such as those in *Silent Screams and Hidden Cries*, the clinician is able to uncover extensive information about the child's cognitive and emotional development that is not generally accessible in the early phases of treatment. This helps define the therapeutic tasks, which include teaching the children the difference between thinking and acting, since this has not been effectively modeled by either the violent or the victimized parent.

Additionally, a therapeutic experience should include a renurturing process in which the therapist plays the role of the "good parent." As demonstrated in their drawings, youngsters from homes in which domestic violence is present frequently suffer from low self-esteem. The therapist is in the ideal position of conveying to the child that someone he or she perceives as important values that child. Another aspect of treatment must include an explanation given to the child, by the therapist, of what is going on in the family (Moore, 1975). This helps to alleviate the child's sense of guilt and confusion, and minimizes his or her distortions. While the youngsters live at the Safe Home, individual treatment is focused around helping them understand the sequence of events that led to their admission.

The mothers whose families of origin were also violent often provide inappropriate parenting. Hershey (1982) found that in many cases, the concepts of physical discipline held by these women met the federal definitions of child abuse. Based on Hershey's study and on clinical work at the Safe Home, including the paucity of nurturance evidenced in the children's drawings, we believe that it is essential that interventions be made with the mothers to improve their parenting and nurturing skills. At the Safe Home, the staff has been facilitating just such groups. The mothers, who are aware of their deficits in this area and have been searching for alternative modes of discipline, are eager to change.

Since the Safe Home guidelines prohibit any hitting of children, the women are encouraged to learn other methods of disciplining, as well as caring for them.

Therapy with the families in the Safe Home is also geared towards facilitating adjustment to a communal setting, and the eventual transition to living in the community, apart from the abuser. The group therapy experience works closely on developing socialization skills and improving self-image, deficits consistently revealed in the children's drawings. Through group and individual therapy, the groundwork is laid for "corrective emotional experiences," in order to help the children form more healthy relationships. Upon discharge, the work is continued by local mental health agencies to which the children are referred. Liaisons are set up throughout the community to facilitate this process. These agencies address the kinds of long-term needs that have been graphically depicted throughout this book.

Although *Silent Screams and Hidden Cries* represents the artwork of only 18 children, and in so doing has limitations in its scope, we believe that these graphics demand attention. The correlation between the family histories and the serious disturbances projected through the children's drawings cannot be ignored. The families who enter the Safe Home tend to be those in the most danger and with the fewest familial, emotional, financial, and community supports. As the statistics in the appendices poignantly delineate, the families represent the most deprived, abused, and chaotic sector of the domestic violence population. This is clear when reviewing the demographic information in the tables, which present information about Safe Home clients in such areas as psychiatric history, child or spouse abuse in the family of origin, income level, alcohol and drug abuse, and the ages of the abused and the abusers. Although people in upper-income brackets do not tend to utilize public agencies, the literature substantiates that in varying degrees, the disorders depicted throughout the book exist in *all* children who witness domestic violence. This includes lower-, middle-, and upper-income families.

It is, therefore, incumbent upon the community to set in motion the systems by which the early detection of domestic violence can be made, the appropriate interventions instituted, and the cyclical effects of violence eradicated. A beginning step is to develop a coordinated effort, through which schools, health centers, physicians, and other local service providers become an integral part of the identification and the subsequent referral of child witnesses. It is essential that the mental health professional community initiate direction towards research into the numbers and the effects of domestic violence on children. Only with a concerted effort by the lay and professional communities can we effectively interrupt the cancerous anguish perpetuated through the generations of domestic violence.

APPENDICES

The following appendices present background information about the children whose drawings are presented in this book, as well as other children and their families who resided in the Safe Home at some time during the two-year period studied.

APPENDIX A

Chart of 18 Children Whose Drawings Are Presented and Their Families

Case Name	Sex	Age	Age of Parents M	Age of Parents F	Religion M	Religion F	Race M	Race F	Income	Education M	Education F	Occupation M	Occupation F	Ethnicity M	Ethnicity F	Drug/Alcohol Abuse M	Drug/Alcohol Abuse F	Marital Status	Abuse in Family of Origin M	Abuse in Family of Origin F	Arrest History M	Arrest History F	Psychiatric Hospitalization M	Psychiatric Hospitalization F	Phys.	Emot.	Sex
Simon	M	8	26	26	P	P	B	B	L	-HS	HS	B/C	B/C	A/A				M	*	*	*	*	*	*			*
Lynn	F	5	37	39	C	C	W	W	L	HS	HS	H/W	R	Pol.			A	M	*					*		*	
Sister	F	13																									
Sister	F	14																									
Ellen	F	6	26	N/A	C	C	B	B	L	-HS	N/A	UE	R	A/A			A	S		*							
Kay	F	5	24	26	P	C	W	W	L	-HS	-HS	H/W	UE	Ir.			D/A	M	*		*			*		*	
Brother	M	3																							*		
Andrew	M	6	25	25	C	P	B	B	L	HS	-HS	H/W	UE	A/A			A	M	*		*					*	
Brother	M	4																							*		
Brother	M	1																									
Ned	M	6	28	29	C	C	W	W	L	HS	-HS	H/W	UE	Ir.			D/A	M	*		*			*		*	
Carol	F	5																									
Lorraine	F	6	27	30	P	P	B	B	L	-C	-C	B/C	B/C	A/A			D/A	M	*		*			*			*
Willy	M	5																									*
Pat	F	9	33	40	C	C	H	H	L	HS	-HS	H/W	B/C	Pr.			A	S	*		*			*			*
Sister	F	15																									*
Sister	F	16																									
Jessica	F	11	30	27	C	C	W	W	L	-C	HS	H/W	B/C	It.	Ir.	A		M	*		*						*
Sister	F	2																									
Brian	M	10	38	39	Baptist		B	B	M	HS	HS	B/C	B/C	A/A				M		*							
James	M	6																									

144

Name	Sex	Age													
Blanche	F	8			C	C	H	L	HS	B/C	Pr.	A	S	* * *	*
Brother	M	5	31	33											
Brother	M	4													
Dennis	M	10	35	38	C	C	W	M	-C	W/C	Ir.	A	M	* *	*
Marilyn	F	8	29	36	C	J	W	M	HS	W/C	G		M	*	*
Miriam	F	5	34	37	C	C	W	L	HS	H/W	B/C	A	D/A M	N/A	
Sister	F	3			C	C	W		-HS	B/C					
Harriet	F	8													
Sister	F	13	29		C	C	B	L	HS	W/C	A/A	A	A M	*	
Sister	F	11	31												
Brother	M	4													

Key

Symbol	Meaning	Symbol	Meaning
M	Mother	R	Retired
F	Father	UE	Unemployed
P	Protestant	H/W	Housewife
C	Catholic	A/A	Afro-American
B	Black	Pol.	Polish
W	White	Ir.	Irish
H	Hispanic	It.	Italian
L	Low Income	Pr.	Puerto Rican
-HS	Never Completed High School	A	Alcohol
HS	Completed High School	D	Drug
-C	Never Completed College	M	Married
C	Completed College	S	Single
B/C	Blue Collar	*	Present
		N/A	Not Available

145

APPENDIX B

Children Residing in the Safe Home
During the Two-Year Period Studied

1) Sex of Children (N=139)

   Females – 41 (1st year)   Males – 31 (1st year)

          <u>35</u> (2nd year)   <u>32</u> (2nd year)

         76   63

2) Ages of Children (N=139)

   Mean age – 4.3

76% of the children were six years of age or under. These figures represent only the ages of the children in the Safe Home and do not include the grown children of Safe Home clients.

Age	# of Children	%
less than 1 yr.	7	5.03
1	23	16.55
2	16	11.51
3	11	7.91
4	20	14.39
5	11	7.91
6	7	5.03
7	6	4.32
8	3	2.16
9	4	2.88
10	21	15.11
11	3	2.16
12	2	1.44
13	3	2.16
14	1	.72
15	1	.72

APPENDIX C

Violence Towards Children

Violence towards children in some form was present in 47 (or 62.4%) of the 77 Safe Home families studied during the two-year period.

Type of Abuse Predominant	# of Children
Physical	31
Emotional	10
Sexual	5
Neglect	1

APPENDIX D

Age of Mothers and Abusers

Age of Mothers

67% of Safe Home women were 30 years of age or under
Mean age of Safe Home client – 25 years

Age	# of Mothers	%
19–21	14	18
22–24	13	16.9
25–27	14	18
28–30	12	15.6
31–33	8	10.4
34–36	6	7.8
37–39	5	6.5
40–45	4	5.2
59	1	1.3

Age of Abuser

50% of men were 30 years of age or younger
Mean age of Safe Home client's abuser – 28 years

APPENDIX E

Religion of Mothers and Abusers

	Mothers		Abusers	
	#	%	#	%
Protestant	26	33.77	19	24.68
Catholic	36	46.75	33	42.86
Jewish	4	5.19	4	5.19
Other	6	7.79	4	5.19
Not available	5	6.49	17	22.08

APPENDIX F

Race of Mothers and Abusers

	Mothers		Abusers	
	#	%	#	%
Black	26	33.8	26	33.8
White	43	55.8	39	50.6
Asian	1	1.3	–	–
Hispanic	7	9.1	8	10.4
Not available	–	–	4	5.2

APPENDIX G

Family Income

	#	%
Low	62	80.5
Middle	15	19.5
Upper	–	–

APPENDIX H

Ethnicity/National Origin of Mothers and Abusers

Ethnicity/National Origin	Mothers	Abusers
Afro-American	9	8
Nigerian	–	1
Trinidadian	1	1
Haitian	3	2
El Salvadorian	1	1
South American	1	2
Puerto Rican	2	3
Polish	1	1
Irish	4	3
German	1	2
Not available	54	53

APPENDIX I

Education of Mothers and Abusers

	Mothers		Abusers	
	#	%	#	%
Less than high school	28	36.3	25	32.47
High school graduate	38	49.3	30	38.96
Some college	5	6.5	–	–
College graduate	4	5.2	4	5.19
Not available	2	2.6	18	23.38

APPENDIX J

Marital Status of Mothers

	#	%
Single	15	19.5
Married	54	70.1
Divorced	6	7.8
Separated	1	1.3
Widowed	1	1.3

APPENDIX K

Length of Relationship of Mothers and Abusers

No. of Years	%
1	10.39
2	10.39
4	20.78
5	12.99
6	7.79
8	15.58
11	7.79
12	5.19
18	1.3
19	1.3
20	2.6
21	1.3
26	1.3
37	1.3

APPENDIX L

Relationship of Abusers to Mothers

	%
Husband	59
Boyfriend	22
Lover's ex-husband	2
Father	4
Mother	2
Not available	11

APPENDIX M

Length of Abuse of Mothers

Years	# of Mothers
Less then 1 Yr.	1
1	3
2	1
3	1
4	3
5	2
8	5
11	2
19	1
37	1
Not available	9

APPENDIX N

Occupation of Mothers and Abusers

Mothers employed outside the home – 31%
Abusers unemployed – 28%

Occupation	Mothers (%)	Abusers (%)
Housewife	62.5	–
Blue Collar	6.2	56.2
White Collar	25	1.6
Unemployed	6.2	18.7
Retired/disabled	–	–
Professional	–	–
Not available	–	23.5

APPENDIX O

Substance Abuse by Mothers and Abusers

Thirty-three percent of mothers and 71% of abusers were involved in some type of substance abuse.

	Mothers (%)	Abusers (%)
Drugs	5.19	10.39
Alcohol	6.49	37.66
Drugs and alcohol	11.69	23.38
Not available	10.39	10.39

APPENDIX P

Arrest History of Mothers and Abusers

	%
Mothers (N=77)	2.6
Abusers (N=77)	23.4

APPENDIX Q

Psychiatric Hospitalizations

	# (N=77)	%
Mothers	12	15.6
Abusers	11	14.3

APPENDIX R

Child or Spouse Abuse in Family of Origin

	# (N=77)	%
Mother's family	31	37.5
Abuser's family	40	56.2

Type of Abuse (N=41)

	Mothers	Abusers
Child	8	5
Wife	1	5
Both	8	8
Not available	1	5

BIBLIOGRAPHY

Abbele, F. *Interpretazioni psicologiche del disegno infantile*. Florence: Edizioni OS, 1970.

American Psychiatric Association. *Diagnostic and statistical manual of mental disorders*, Third Edition. Washington: American Psychiatric Association, 1980.

Bolander, K. *Assessing personality through tree drawings*. New York: Basic Books, 1977.

Bowen, M. *Family therapy and clinical practice*. New York: Jason Aronson, 1978.

Bowlby, J. *Violence in the family as a disorder of attachment of the care giving system*. Paper presented at Karen Horney Psychological Association, New York City, 1983.

Brown, A., Pelkowitz, D., & Kaplan, S. *Child witnesses of family violence: A study of psychological correlates*. Paper presented at American Psychological Association, Anaheim, CA, 1983.

Buck, J. *The House-Tree-Person technique*. Los Angeles, CA: Western Psychological Services, 1981.

Burns, R. C. *Self-growth in families: Kinetic family drawings research and application*. New York: Brunner/Mazel, 1982.

Burns, R. C., & Kaufman, S. H. *Action, styles and symbols in kinetic family drawings: An interpretative manual*. New York: Brunner/Mazel, 1972.

Burt, C. *Mental and scholastic tests*. London: P. S. King & Son, 1921.

Crevel, van N. *But what about the kids?* A paper about possibilities and impossibilities to help the battered wife's child during its stay in the Refuge of "Blijf van m'n Lijf." Amsterdam, June 1976.

163

Di Leo, J. H. *Children's drawings as diagnostic aids.* New York: Brunner/Mazel, 1973.

Di Leo, J. H. *Interpreting children's drawings.* New York: Brunner/Mazel, 1983.

Erikson, E. H. *Childhood and society.* New York: W. W. Norton, 1963.

Freud, S. (1938). Three essays on sexuality. In J. Strachey (Ed.), *Standard Edition*, Vol. 7. London: Hogarth Press, 1950.

Goodenough, F. *Measurement of intelligence by drawings.* New York: Harcourt, Brace and World, 1926.

Griffith, R. *A study of imagination in early childhood.* London: Paul Kegan Trench, Trubnero Co., 1935.

Haley, J. *Problem solving therapy.* San Francisco: Jossey-Bass, 1976.

Hammer, E. *The clinical application of projective drawings.* Springfield, IL: Charles C Thomas, 1980.

Harris, D. *Children's drawings as measures of intellectual maturity.* New York: Harcourt Brace Jovanovich, 1963.

Hershey, D. *Domestic violence: Children reared in explosive homes.* Paper presented at Eastern Psychological Association, Baltimore, MD, April 1982.

Hughes, H. M. Brief interventions with children in a battered women's shelter: A model preventive program. *Family Relations*, 1982, *31*, 495–502.

Jolles, I. *The catalogue for the qualitative interpretation of the House-Tree-Person.* Los Angeles: Western Psychological Services, 1971.

Kellogg, R. *Analyzing children's art.* Palo Alto, CA: Mayfield Publishing, 1970.

Klepsch, M., & Logie, L. *Children draw and tell. An introduction to the uses of children's human figure drawings.* New York: Brunner/Mazel, 1982.

Koch, C. *The tree test.* New York: Grune & Stratton, 1952.

Koppitz, E. *Psychological evaluation of children's drawings.* New York: Grune & Stratton, 1968.

Landisberg, S. Variations and applications. In J. Buck & E. Hammer (Eds.), *Advances in the House-Tree-Person technique.* Los Angeles: Western Psychological Services, 1969.

Levine, M. B. Interparental violence and its effect on the children: A study of fifty families in general practice. *Medicine Science Law*, 1975, *15*, 172–176.

Luquet, G. H. *Les dessins d'un enfant: Étude psychologique.* Paris: Librairie Félix Alcan, 1913.

Machover, K. *Personality projection in the human figure.* Springfield, IL: Charles C Thomas, 1980.

Maslow, A. H. *Motivation and personality.* New York: Harper, 1954.

Minuchin, S. *Family therapy techniques.* Cambridge, MA: Harvard University Press, 1981.

Moore, J. G. Yo-yo children – Victims of matrimonial violence. *Child Welfare*, 1975, *8*, 557–566.

O'Brien, R. P., & Patton, W. F. Development of an objective scoring method for Kinetic Family Drawings. *Journal of Personality Assessment*, 1974, *58*, 156–164.

Ogdon, D. P. *Psychodiagnostics and personality assessment: A handbook*. Los Angeles: Western Psychological Services, 1981.

Pfouts, J., Schopler, J., & Henley, H. C. Forgotten victims of family violence. *Social Work* 1982, *27*(4), 367–368.

Porter, B., & O'Leary, K. D. Marital discord and childhood behavior problems. *Journal of Abnormal Child Psychiatry*, 1980, *8*(3), 692–699.

Rosenbaum, A., & O'Leary, K. D. The unintended victims of marital violence. *American Journal of Orthopsychiatry*, 1981, *51*(4), 692–694.

Satir, V. *Conjoint family therapy* (15th ed.). Palo Alto, CA: Science and Behavior Books, 1967.

Shapiro, D. *Neurotic styles*. New York: Basic Books, 1965.

Straus, M., Gelles, R., & Steinmetz, S. *Behind closed doors: Violence in the American family*. Garden City, NY: Anchor Books/Doubleday, 1981.

Urban, W. H. *The Draw-a-Person catalogue for interpretive analysis*. Los Angeles: Western Psychological Services, 1963.

INDEX OF
CHILDREN'S DRAWINGS

Child's Name	Drawings	Pages
Andrew	P2, H2	16, 86
Blanche	P13, H13, T6	40, 106, 126
Brian	P10, F8, H10, T5	32, 70, 100, 124
Carol	P3, F3, H3	18, 58, 88
Dennis	P14, H14, T7	42, 108, 128
Ellen	F5	60
Harriet	P9, F7, H9, T4	30, 66, 98, 122
James	P11, F9, H11	36, 72, 102
Jessica	P8, H8, T3	28, 96, 120
Kay	P1, F2, H1	14, 56, 84
Lorraine	P5, F10, H6, H7, T2	22, 74, 94, 95, 118
Lynn	F1	54
Marilyn	P15, F11, H15, T8	46, 76, 110, 132
Miriam	F12	78
Ned	P4, F4, H5	20, 59, 92
Pat	P7, F6, H4	26, 64, 90
Simon	P12, H12, T1	40, 104, 116
Willy	P6	24

Note: The following is a key to the above abbreviations:

Human Figure Drawing	P
Kinetic Family Drawing	F
Tree Drawing	T
House Drawing	H

GENERAL INDEX

169

170

Fathers
  Conduct Disorders among sons of, 136
  in human figure drawings, 28
  in kinetic family drawings, 52
  see also Abusers
Feet, 22
  in kinetic family drawings, 64, 70
Female children
  helplessness and depression among, 136–37
  identification with victim by, 4
Fingers
  in human figure drawings, 34
  see also Arms; Hands
Flowers, in tree drawings, 132, 134
Food, in kinetic family drawings, 54
Freud, Sigmund, 6
Fruits, in tree drawings, 116, 118

Gelles, R., 48
Goodenough, F., 36
Goodenough and Harris Drawing Test scores, 13
Grandparents, in kinetic family drawings, 56, 60–62
Grass
  in house drawings, 106
  in tree drawings, 126
Group therapy, 138

Hair, in human figure drawings, 34, 36, 42
Haley, J., 50
Hammer, E., 7–8
  on bodies, 74
  on detailing in drawings, 9
  on human figure drawings, 11, 22, 28, 34
  on tree drawings, 113, 126
Hands, xvi, 22, 26
  in human figure drawings, 28, 34
  in kinetic family drawings, 54, 70
Harris, D., 7
Heads, in kinetic family drawings, 54, 58
Health condition of children, 4–5
Helplessness
  among female children, 136–37
  in human figure drawings, 18, 20, 22, 28
  in kinetic family drawings, 68
Heroic figures, 38
Hershey, D., 135–36

Holes, in tree drawings, 114, 120, 124, 126, 130, 132
Hospitalizations (psychiatric) of mothers and abusers, 161
House drawings, xiv, 79–81
  samples of, 82–112
House-Tree-Person (HTP) Test, xiv–xv
Human figures, 11–13
  in family drawings, 49–78
  samples of, 14–48

I.Q. scores, 13
Income of abused families, 138, 151
Infants, 4–5

Jolles, I. 9, 11
  on house drawings, 81, 106
  on human figure drawings, 26, 34, 42
  on transparency, in house drawings, 112
  on tree drawings, 116
Jumping ropes, in human figure drawings, 46

Kaplan, S., 137
Kaufman, S.H., 46, 49–51, 56
Kellogg, R., 90
Kinetic family drawings, 49–52
  samples of, 54–78
Koch, C., 113
Koppitz. E.
  on clouds in human figure drawings, 42
  on house drawings, 102
  on human figure drawings, 11–13, 16, 34, 38, 42
  on kinetic family drawings, 66

Leaves, 56
Legs, in kinetic family drawings, 54, 62, 64
Lines, 7
  quality of, 10
  in tree drawings, 122
Living rooms, in house drawings, 112
Localized scribbling, 7
Luquet, G.H., xvi

Machover, K., 11, 28
Male children
  aggression in, 4
  Conduct Disorders among, 136